DBT SKILLS GUIDEBOOK FOR TEENS

Transform Stress and Emotional Chaos into Control
and Connection
A Teen's Guide to Thriving through Mindfulness,
Regulation, and Relationship Skills

Emma Davis

Impact
— PUBLISHING —

TABLE OF CONTENT

Introduction . . . . *v*

Chapter 1   Navigating Your Inner World 1

Chapter 2   Thriving In Your Environment .19

Chapter 3   Crafting Your Ideal Life. 31

Chapter 4   Mastering Your Relationships .52

Chapter 5   Conquering Your Inner Demons 68

Chapter 6   Rising Above Trauma 82

Chapter 7   Unleashing Your Potential 103

Chapter 8   Sustaining Your Growth 114

Chapter 9   Envisage Your Future 128

Chapter 10 Embracing Your Best Self. 142

Conclusion *158*

About the Author *162*

Bibliography *165*

Page left blank intentionally

INTRODUCTION

"Within you, there is a stillness and a sanctuary to which you can retreat at any time and be yourself."
           - Hermann Hesse

DID YOU KNOW that experiencing peace of mind does not always mean your life is joyous? Ever feel like you're on a rollercoaster – emotions zooming up and down faster than you can say "homework deadline"? School drama, friend troubles, the never-ending pressure to be perfect – it's enough to make anyone's head spin. But wait! There's a secret power hidden in you. It's a place of calm, a quiet refuge you can visit anytime, even during the craziest day.

This book is your guide to awakening that power inside you. It's all about D.B.T. skills, a toolbox packed with techniques to help you navigate the ups and downs of teen life.

Forget chasing some imaginary state of constant happiness. Peace of mind, even with the chaos, is totally achievable. Let's dive in and discover how to appreciate the "here and now," even when the "now" feels a little overwhelming.

When we talk about growth, teenage life is the best example. These years are like the building stage of your life — the time when you build the new you. Your body is changing in more than one way. Your feelings are all over the place. You are figuring out who you are and what you want in your life. Well, to be honest, it is a super exciting time of life. But at the same time, it can be the most confusing and overwhelming period.

On the one hand, your brain is going through intense training. You are getting better at thinking logically, understanding emotions, and forming connections with others. It's kind of like upgrading your level in a video game. With each passing year, you unlock different skills and abilities.

This is when you start asking yourself a lot of questions. Like, who are you? What do you believe? What do you want to do when you grow up? It's kind of tricky to figure all this out, you know?

But then again, all these changes can be like a big puzzle. One moment, you might feel amazing, and the next, you might feel sad or annoyed. It's totally normal to have all sorts of feelings during this time, but sometimes, they can feel strong and hard to handle.

You might also feel a bit awkward about your body changing or like you don't fit in anywhere. That's okay too! Everyone goes through stuff like that during their teenage years.

The cool thing is that you're not alone. Most teens face challenges, but with a little help, you can totally handle them. Just remember, being a teenager is about growing and discovering. It's okay if things seem messy sometimes. There will be good times and not-so-good times, but with support, you can totally navigate through this exciting phase and become the awesome person you're meant to be!

Well, when talking about emotions, the most common thing that hits the mind is teenage love. It is wild. It's like riding a rollercoaster of emotions, right? One moment, you're on cloud nine, and the next, your stomach feels like it's hosting a butterfly mosh pit. It's totally normal! But here's the deal — all those wild hormones, feelings, and changes happening together can make things a bit intense.

When you have a crush on someone or are in a relationship, your brain releases chemicals like dopamine and oxytocin. They give you that happy, excited, warm-and-fuzzy feeling. But sometimes, that mix can also bring on not-so-fun stuff like anxiety, feeling down, or even obsessive thoughts. It's like your brain is on a sugar rush, and controlling the ups and downs can be tricky.

Teens often deal with relationship challenges, and the mix of emotions, changes, and hormones linked to teenage love can amplify negative feelings, mental health issues, and obsessive thinking. This book helps teens address those issues.

Dealing with relationships during your teenage years can be a really difficult task. You know you're dealing with all sorts of emotions, changes in your body, and those pesky hormones that sometimes make you feel like a fool.

When it comes to teenage love, these factors can sometimes trigger negative feelings and mental health struggles and even lead to a situation of obsessive thinking, which is not good news for youngsters.

But hey, there's good news! There is something that can help, something specifically designed to help teens like you tackle these challenges head-on.

This book will help you handle all the ups and downs of teenage love and relationships. It's like having a cool older sibling or a wise friend who's been through it all before. It will act like a friendly guide that offers advice, support, and strategies for dealing with all the troubles of love and relationships.

Let me break it down for you. Imagine that you're head over heels for someone, but things get rocky. Maybe you start feeling anxious, sad, or even obsessed with thoughts about someone special.

And trust me, I'm not joking. It's quite common. Studies show that around 30% of teens deal with anxiety disorders, and a big reason for that is often linked to relationship challenges and the stress of handling teenage love.

This book dives into real stories from teens, offering tips on communication, setting boundaries, and self-care, and even includes exercises to help you grasp your emotions more clearly. It will be like a road map to healthy relationships and a happier, more confident you!

The best and most effective solution to all these problems lies in a simple thing: D.B.T. skills, which stands for Dialectical Behavior Therapy. It might sound a bit fancy, but it's straightforward and helpful for everyday life. It's all about learning useful skills you can use every day.

With D.B.T., you undergo a structured program over a few weeks or months. This program includes group sessions with others and one-on-one chats with a therapist. The way it's set up might change based on what you need help with, such as anxiety or something else.

The word "dialectical" basically means looking at things from different sides. D.B.T. believes there can be more than one way to see a situation. For example, feelings can be valid, but they can also sometimes get in the way. Or someone can be doing their best but still have room to improve.

D.B.T. helps with thinking better and doing positive stuff. It also borrows techniques from Eastern practices, like mindfulness and self-compassion.

One cool thing about D.B.T. is that it combines different methods, even ones that seem different. It helps you accept things as they are while also working to make changes. This helps tackle lots of different challenges at once, unlike some other therapies that focus on just one thing.

D.B.T. helps with tons of stuff. We will discuss it in detail but let me share some basic functions with you.

1. **Handling emotions better:** D.B.T. shows you how to name your feelings, understand why they happen, and deal with them without getting stuck. It also helps you to have more good experiences in your life.

2. **Stopping impulsive actions:** Sometimes, when feelings are tough, people do things without thinking. D.B.T. teaches calming tricks and accepting tough feelings so you aren't impulsive.

3. **Making relationships better:** D.B.T. teaches you how to communicate better with others, like being understanding and honest, setting boundaries, and speaking up for yourself.

4. **Figuring out who you are:** With D.B.T., you can learn mindfulness and balance your feelings and thoughts. This helps you get to know yourself more and figure out where you fit in the world.

D.B.T. skills are great for understanding what's really going on inside you, especially with your emotions. We all know how emotions can be tricky, right? One moment, you're super happy, and the next, you're feeling frustrated or down. Well, D.B.T. is like training to be a feelings detective!

Life can get loud sometimes, making it tough to listen to what's happening inside. D.B.T. skills can help you hit the pause button and take a moment to be present. Just picture yourself taking deep breaths and focusing on what's happening around you right now. By calming down, you can start to recognize your emotions better.

Let's say you've hit pause and noticed a jumble of emotions. What are they? D.B.T. helps you put a name to those feelings. Are you feeling nervous about a big test? Sad because you had a fight with a friend? Frustrated because your little brother keeps borrowing your stuff? Naming your feelings helps you understand them.

Did you know your body can tell you a lot about your emotions? D.B.T. teaches you to be a detective for your body's clues, too! Is your heart racing when you're feeling stressed? Maybe your stomach clenches when you're anxious? By paying attention to these physical signs, you can recognize your emotions even earlier.

Research indicates that teens who learn D.B.T. skills are more adept at managing their emotions. They exhibit less impulsive behavior during overwhelming moments and recover from tough situations quickly.

Think of it like this: the more you understand your emotions, the better you can deal with them. It's like having a toolbox full of cool skills to navigate your feelings and make life a little less stressful. Pretty neat, right?

Well, I have been working with teens for over a decade now. I have witnessed them deal with all sorts of emotional stuff. I have seen firsthand how tough things can be for them, and that's what pushed me to write this book.

This book is tailored for YOU! It's filled with practical tips and tricks based on real-life experiences that will help you navigate the ups and downs of teenage life. Consider these pages a toolkit full of skills to build your emotional strength and the ability to tackle anything life throws your way.

I won't sugarcoat it; emotions can be really confusing. But this book is all about giving you effective, actionable steps that can change the game of your emotional struggle. You won't find any fancy jargon or anything like that, just real talk and proven methods to help you manage your feelings in a healthy way.

So, whether you are feeling stressed, anxious, scared, or simply overwhelmed, this book is here to pull you back from that emotional trance. It's all about giving you the gear you need to feel content with your life. It will make you more confident about yourself and your abilities, making you the best version of yourself.

> *"The greatest weapon against stress is our ability to choose one thought over another."*
>
> **– William James**

It is said that you are your greatest weapon against stress and emotional problems in any relationship, but only if you can choose one thought at a time or over another.

You must have heard the saying that you are your own best defense against stress or emotional challenges in relationships. But what does that really mean? Well, it's all about your power to choose one thought over another.

To make it easier, imagine that you are in an argument with a friend or a family member. In this situation, your mind might start racing with negative thoughts like, "They don't care about me" or "I'll never be able to resolve this."

These types of gloomy thoughts are hazardous for your mental and emotional health. They might make you feel more stressed and upset about the situation, and you will start overanalyzing every small thing, such as, "Will they talk to me again?" What if they end their friendship over this?" "Will I be left all alone?". This overthinking will make it more difficult for you to sort out the situation.

But here's the thing – you can choose a different thought. Instead of dwelling on those negative ideas, you can choose to focus on something positive, and who knows, you might find a way to solve the issue constructively.

It's like flipping a switch in your mind from "I can't handle this" to "I can find a way through this." Research has proven that our thoughts have a powerful impact on our emotions and well-being. For example, studies in psychology say that positive thinking is a strong force that can be a whole game changer.

So, the next time you find yourself in a stressful situation or facing emotional challenges in a relationship, remember that you have the power to choose your thoughts. By shifting to more positive and constructive thinking, you can be your own ally in overcoming stress and building healthier relationships.

I know it all sounds overwhelming, and yes, it can be challenging if not managed properly.

But don't worry! I've got your back.

In this book, you will learn each and every essential skill and technique that will empower you to regulate your emotions perfectly and strategically. So, without overthinking it, turn to the next page and take a peek into the world of D.B.T. with me. Together, we will change the gameplay of your teenage life.

CHAPTER 1

Navigating Your Inner World

> *"Mindfulness is not difficult. We just need to remember to do it."*
>
> **– Sharon Salzberg**

MASTERING YOUR OWN mind is one of the most important things you can do in life. As Sharon Salzberg said, "being mindful doesn't need to be difficult – it's just a matter of choice". Making that choice can have a huge impact, especially for teens dealing with stressful times.

Did you know that research shows that nearly half of teens feel extremely stressed on a daily basis? All that pressure we put on ourselves can really take a toll on our mental health and relationships. But there are skills we can learn to help us cope in a much healthier way. One approach that's been shown to be highly effective is called Dialectical Behavior Therapy, or DBT for short.

DBT was originally developed to help people dealing with severe emotional dysregulation and borderline personality disorder. Strategies like mindfulness, interpersonal effectiveness, and distress tolerance teach concrete techniques to stay in control of your reactions and emotions even during tough situations. Studies have found that DBT can significantly reduce stress, anxiety, and depressive symptoms for both teens and adults.

In this chapter, we'll take a closer look at what DBT involves and how simple practices like mindfulness can reap big rewards. We'll explore the science behind how techniques like deep breathing help calm the body's natural "fight or flight" response to stress. I'll also share some straightforward DBT skills you can start using right away to help cope with everyday problems in a balanced, non-reactive way. My hope is that learning these skills equips you with powerful mental tools to face challenges with more clarity and peace of mind.

Understanding DBT and Exploring Mindfulness

We all have those days where our feelings seem too intense, whether it's anger, sadness, or anxiety. It can feel overwhelming. The good news is there are proven ways to get better at handling emotions, even on tough days.

DBT was created in the 1970s and has helped a lot of people manage their behaviors and improve relationships. It teaches techniques to stay calm and in control of your reactions.

What is DBT?

DBT takes a balanced approach - it supports you where you're at but also encourages positive change. Initially made for severe emotions, now it helps things like depression, too. And the best part is that anyone can benefit from its tools!

How do DBT Skills Work?

We all have days where everything feels like a battle. Navigating feelings, people, and outside pressures makes you tired just thinking about it. But what if there was a way to boost your mental game without a phone booth? DBT provides training to build strength, speed, and toughness when life gets hard.

Through interactive activities focusing on four core techniques, aka "pillars," you'll discover weapons to pause crazy thoughts and calm down fast. You'll gain strength to face stress without cracking. Fiery emotions won't overpower you thanks to breathing powers. Relationships that cause stress become no sweat with people skills.

Curious about these super skills? Let's dive into DBT's four pillars of power and how they'll make you feel unstoppable!

The 4 Pillars of DBT for Teens

DBT provides awesome tools for the ups and downs of life. The core focuses on four "pillars" skills that are super fun to learn in group activities. Let's check them out!

Pillar 1 - Mindfulness

Research shows mindfulness can literally change your brain for the better. One study found areas linked to managing emotions grew in just eight weeks! Mindfulness means hitting pause when feelings get intense.

Wasn't that a chill way to briefly relax and notice your surroundings? Over time, mindfulness challenges like that can train your brain to stay present even when things get hairy. It helps you focus on what you want to think about and avoid unwanted thoughts. Pretty neat, right?

With practice, it gets easier to separate yourself from unhelpful thoughts.

> *"You are not your thoughts; you are the observer of your thoughts." - Amit Ray, Mindfulness Living in the Moment*   **- Living in the Breath**

Put Your Mindfulness Powers to the Test!

You just learned thaZt mindfulness can change your brain structure in just two months. But how can you experience these benefits for yourself right now? Let's do a quick challenge to prove the effectiveness of mindfulness.

I call this one the "5 Senses Scavenger Hunt." Set a timer for 5 minutes and simply observe the world around you using each of your five senses, one at a time. I'll start...

Sight: I notice the trees blowing outside the window, colorful artwork on the wall, and shapes and patterns all around.

Now it's your turn! Focus on sounds. What can you hear in the immediate environment? Clocks ticking, people chatting nearby, music faintly playing?

Next is touch. How does your chair or floor feel beneath you? What is the temperature of the air? Are your hands in your lap?

Smell is next. Take a slow, deep breath. Are any scents detectable, like food or flowers in bloom?

Finally, there is taste. Pay attention to any flavors in your mouth — minty gum or the taste of your drink.

And.... That's it!

Pillar 2 - Distress Tolerance

Ever wanna yell, "This isn't fair!" when sad or anxious? Radical acceptance means seeing tough situations as they are versus how we want them. One activity shows how small issues seem years later and puts things in perspective!

The goal with distress tolerance is riding emotional waves instead of drowning in them with destructive behaviors like screaming when mad. As Maya Angelou said,

"I can deal with pain, but I cannot stand still in the face of injustice."

Pillar 3 - Emotion Regulation

Notice certain feelings trigger behaviors like snapping or isolating? DBT helps spot these patterns and pick healthier responses. Feeling angry? Try relaxing your body with deep breathing instead of hostility. Or if sad, calling a buddy releases feel-good brain chemicals just like exercise!

Pillar 4 - Interpersonal Effectiveness

Relationships bring joy and stress, but communication techniques from DBT make getting along easier. There's this funny exercise acting out towels being folded - it practices asserting needs politely! "I feel" statements share feelings without blaming others. As the saying goes:

"Alone, we can do so little; together, we can do so much."

These four pillars give you pro mental skills to handle anything life throws your way. The techniques help ride highs and weather lows with more balance and toughness!

It might be shocking to hear, but almost 10% of Americans over the age of 18 meet the criteria for Borderline Personality Disorder (BPD), which causes impairment similar to PTSD, bipolar disorder, and depression. However, researchers found that after one year of DBT treatment, nearly 75% of BPD patients no longer qualified for the diagnosis. DBT helps "rewire" thought and emotional patterns that are maladaptive through structured skill-building over time.

A powerful way DBT cultivates mindfulness is by practicing wise mind acceptance. This means noticing emotions, thoughts, or urges without reacting and allowing them to pass rather than fighting internal experiences that fuel further distress. In other words, accept what is and respond in an effective way.

For example, when feeling irritated before an exam, one may acknowledge the feeling is present and then deliberately shift attention toward calming a rapid heartbeat through focused breathing instead of anxiously ruminating. Wise mind acceptance fosters composure in challenging situations we cannot immediately change.

STRENGTHEN YOUR BONDS WITH DBT COMMUNICATION SKILLS

Ever wish there was an easier way to share important needs with friends without damaging relationships? DBT's got you.

- It teaches asserting respectfully through "I feel" statements instead of blaming. Compromising while keeping self-respect too. Saying no firmly when required. Addressing conflicts constructively keeps things healthy.
- Studies found these interpersonal effectiveness tools significantly cut down on partner violence risks. Win-win!
- According to research, while changes may not happen fast, regular DBT practice tends to have long-lasting positive effects on mood, stress and control. By mastering inner experiences, you can roll with life's highs and lows with more confidence.

Give DBT relationship skills a shot. Over time, you'll cultivate the balance of acceptance and change needed to deepen important bonds stronger than ever before.

The Evidence of the Science Behind DBT Skills

In today's world, stress and a lack coping strategies are super common problems for teens. As a mental wellness advocate, I've talked a lot about DBT being awesome. But opinions alone don't cut it - we need facts backing important claims.

So, I looked at research proving why DBT deserves recognition. What I found made me even more sure everyone should learn these inner balance techniques. Here are some key facts:

Research found that DBT reduces suicide attempts and self-harm among at-risk youth. Just mindfulness alone was proven through brain scans to change emotional control areas after weekly sessions.

Extra studies confirm that DBT lowered depression and anxiety symptoms plus better school performance in long-term versus short-term fixes. Strong proof it's invaluable!

How DBT Revolutionized Treatment

Creator Marsha Linehan combined strategies through trial and error to address struggles without judgment. Compared to other therapies, it cut dropout rates hugely and saved lives. Refined over decades, it's proven effective worldwide.

DBT's power comes from meeting people where they're at, not criticizing, to guide healing and hope. Facts show it truly equips teens with skills to handle life's challenges.

REMODEL YOUR BRAIN FOR CALM WITH DBT

Ever feel like stress and worries are always nagging away at you? Good news - DBT can tweak your brain to handle pressures better. Studies show mindfulness grows control centers while settling stress zones. Exposure therapy in DBT sessions helped desensitize fear areas too. Over time, prefrontal tweaks stayed put as proof of how skills rewire your circuitry.

Validation in DBT may undo harsh past experiences' neural scars. Non-judgment from therapists calmed cortisol responses linked to shame. Over time, this cognitive recalibration likely rebuilds more compassionate neural networks.

Two months of mindfulness shifted teens' maps toward self-control hubs and away from sadness sites. No wonder participants felt a new sense of command!

Give DBT a shot. Grounding, distress tolerance and emotion regulation provide superpowers to face anything high school throws. I promise practicing these moves will cultivate rocksteady resilience from within. You've totally got this!

The Mindful Teen

Dealing with intense feelings is super common for teens but can feel impossible. Studies show mental health issues like depression, anxiety, and self-harm are more normal than you think during these years. The good news? DBT was made just for you!

As a proven therapy, DBT has been shown to really help conditions lots of teens face, like mood disorders, cutting, and eating issues. It does this by teaching you skills to rein in wild emotions and behaviors for good.

For example, mindfulness training uses deep breathing and grounding techniques proven to calm your "worry brain" when you start to spiral. This helps you feel chill and in control. DBT also tackles impulsiveness through strategies like squeezing an ice cube when mad or sad instead of harming yourself.

If bad feelings lead to unhealthy coping, DBT provides better options to break those patterns. Through emotional skills and a caring therapist, it gets to the root of pain so you can build up balanced ways of dealing that don't hurt you or others. Stories from teens who used DBT show it 100% works to make emotions way more manageable.

By being open-minded and trying out DBT, you have only good things to gain in getting free from the mental turmoil holding you back. Your well-being is totally worth it, so ask trusted adults like a counselor about giving it a shot. With time and committing to the process, DBT will empower you to steer your mental health ship steadily even during wild storms inside.

BOOST YOUR SKILLS AND SUPPORT SYSTEM WITH DBT

Core Elements:

- *Individual Therapy* - Get personalized guidance from your therapist to apply coping strategies.
- *Group Classes* - Attend skill-building sessions with peers led by experts in mindfulness, distress tolerance and more. Studies show the social aspect increases motivation and learning.
- *Phone Coaching* - Your therapist is available by phone between appointments to help you manage real-life situations as they occur.
- *Collaborative Consultation* - Participate as your provider continuously improves the DBT approach by discussing cases with colleagues.

This complete system maximizes results through customized attention, peer connections and non-stop enhancements.

Try it out - with DBT's comprehensive support network, you've got everything you need working together for positive change!

Getting Started with DBT Techniques

Now that the DBT basics are clear, it's time to try out valuable skills. Even simple tools over time can totally shift your mindset through dedicated practice. Challenges become way more manageable once you commit. The journey is as rewarding as it is challenging - these techniques truly empower lasting wellness from within.

Tips for Teens Learning DBT

DBT provides proven techniques to regulate intense feelings and handle stressful situations better. Here are some easy ways to start incorporating skills:

Getting Into Mindfulness

Mindfulness trains you to live fully in the present versus worrying over the past or future. To practice:
- Set phone reminders for 5 to 10 min daily mindfulness like deep breathing.
- Apps like Calm or Headspace make guided sessions simple.
- Notice small details around you to keep your brain present.

Using Distress Tolerance

When emotions feel overwhelming, distress tolerance helps you ride the wave instead of making it bigger. Try:
- Holding an ice cube and focusing on how it feels to distract from stress or anger.
- Squeezing your hands tightly to release physical tension.
- Listening to chill music to shift your thinking.

Understanding Emotions

Emotion regulation involves understanding your feelings, so you guide actions, not just react. Develop these skills by:
- Keeping a journal to identify emotion patterns.
- Using a feelings chart to label tricky emotions.
- Practicing positive self-talk to challenge unhelpful thoughts fueling bad feelings.

Improving Relationships

Interpersonal effectiveness builds healthier bonds. Try to incorporate the following to improve your relationships:
- Assertiveness training to communicate needs with confidence.
- Active listening when others share to show you care.
- Negotiation strategies that work for everyone involved.

Stick with regular practice - these skills truly get easier over time!

Don't get discouraged by commitment. You've got this!

What is PLEASE, and How Can it Help?

Feeling super emotional? There's a simple technique called PLEASE that can seriously help manage feelings. PLEASE stands for basic needs that fuel your mental armor. When needs are met, staying chill during stress gets way easier.

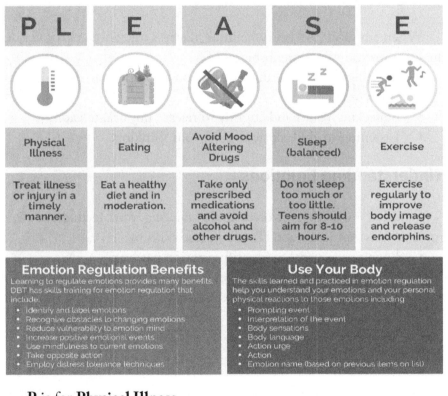

P L Physical Illness	E Eating	A Avoid Mood Altering Drugs	S Sleep (balanced)	E Exercise
Treat illness or injury in a timely manner.	Eat a healthy diet and in moderation.	Take only prescribed medications and avoid alcohol and other drugs.	Do not sleep too much or too little. Teens should aim for 8-10 hours.	Exercise regularly to improve body image and release endorphins.

Emotion Regulation Benefits	Use Your Body
Learning to regulate emotions provides many benefits. DBT has skills training for emotion regulation that include: • Identify and label emotions • Recognize obstacles to changing emotions • Reduce vulnerability to emotion mind • Increase positive emotional events • Use mindfulness to current emotions • Take opposite action • Employ distress tolerance techniques	The skills learned and practiced in emotion regulation help you understand your emotions and your personal physical reactions to those emotions including • Prompting event • Interpretation of the event • Body sensations • Body language • Action urge • Action • Emotion name (based on previous items on list)

P is for **Physical Illness**

How you feel physically affects your mind a ton. Treat any issues for less struggle handling tough times.

L is for **Listening to Your Body**

Rest and activity should match how you truly feel each day through self-care. That arms you for life challenges.

E is for Balanced Eating

I know moods mess with appetites but fueling right lifts mood and the feeling of being in control. Little changes like daily fruit is very beneficial.

A is for **Avoiding Substances**

Alcohol and excess caffeine/nicotine mess with clear thinking. Stay substance-free to try calmer coping strategies when down. Your brain will say thanks!

S is for **Quality Sleep**

Research shows that most of us don't clock the needed 8 hours! Optimize your schedule and stuff for better rest. Mental wellness loves a good night's rest.

E is for **Exercise**

Do what you enjoy – lifting, dancing, sports? Movement pumps up happy brain chemicals majorly.

Caring for basics through PLEASE strengthens your mental game. It may seem minor but countless folks improved their wellbeing from the inside out when they committed. Give yourself an upgrade and see what happens!

The DEAR MAN System

Hey, are you tired of stressful talks that leave you drained or relationships that feel disconnected? Well, then, you need to hear about this secret weapon for saving any situation — it's called DEAR MAN, and it's about to become your new BFF.

A simple set of tricks will turn any heated debate into a healthy discussion, paving the way for stronger bonds. I'm dying to spill the deets on this low-key genius strategy, so pull up a chair because your mind is about to be blown!

BOOST YOUR SKILLS AND SUPPORT SYSTEM WITH DEARMAN: A KILLPROOF CONFLICT RESOLUTION TECHNIQUE

Wanna practice effective communication and get what you want? **Try this DEARMAN roleplay activity** with a friend:

Choose a typical disagreement you've had, like curfew or chores. Take turns using the DEARMAN structure to roleplay the discussion as positive and productive as possible:

D - Describe the issue objectively

E - Express your feelings with "I statement"

A - Assert clearly what you need

R - Reinforce the benefits of the agreement

M - Stay mindful and focused

A - Ask for their perspective

N - Negotiate a mutually agreeable solution

Practicing these research-backed steps in a low-stakes scenario makes them easier IRL. See how effectively you can understand each other's POV and resolve conflicts now! Communication mastery, here you come.

IMPROVE COMMUNICATION

Using the DEARMAN Template

STEP-BY-STEP GUIDE TO GETTING WHAT YOU WANT

DESCRIBE
- Describe the current situation.
- Stick to the facts.
- Clarify what you are reacting to.

EXPRESS
- Express your opinions, feelings, and interpretations of the situation
- Don't assume the other person knows.
- Use "I" statements instead of "you" statements.

ASSERT
- Ask for what you want or say no clearly.
- Do not assume that others will know what you want from this interaction.

REINFORCE
- Describe natural consequences, whether a reward or a negative consequence.
- Tell the person what would happen if you got what you wanted.

BE MINDFUL
- Keep your focus on your goals.
- Don't get off topic.
- Keep repeating E or A section as needed.

APPEAR CONFIDENT
- Appear effective and confident.
- Use a confident tone and physical manner.

NEGOTIATE
- Offer and ask for other solutions to the problem if necessary.
- Focus on what will work.

CBT California @Marsha Linehan

Troubleshooting Teen Troubles

Being a teen comes with challenges, but I learned some simple strategies that got me through. Now, I'm passing them on to help you all, too!

1. Stay Positive

When things go wrong, look for the good instead of just the bad. Optimism boosts how fast you bounce back.

2. Build Toughness

We all mess up - that's how you grow. Face problems head-on so you become even stronger. Don't fear mistakes.

3. Lean on Your Crew

Friends and fam hold you down through thick and thin. Share what's bugging you to lift that weight off your shoulders.

4. Find What You Love

Interests keep you driven when times are tough. Try new stuff to maybe discover cool talents you didn't know about.

5. Map Out Goals

Plan what you want to achieve so it feels less scary. Break big dreams into smaller steps to check off along the way.

6. Schedule Your Time

Life gets hectic, so organize tasks without burning out. Also, schedule fun time - everyone needs balance!

7. Take Care of Yourself

Fuel right, sleep enough, and get moving - it arms you to handle stress way better. Little acts like meditation also help a ton.

8. It's Okay To Mess Up

We all make mistakes - it's how you learn. Use errors to improve, like most successful folks had to do too.

9. Surround Yourself With Good Vibes

True friends lift you way higher than negativity could bring down. Seek out an encouraging crew.

10. Trust Your Gut

Only you decide your path. Make choices that feel right to you. Standing up for yourself builds confidence.

No matter what comes up, remember that you've totally got this! I believe in you all.

Key Takeaways

- DBT skills like mindfulness, distress tolerance, emotion regulation, and interpersonal effectiveness can help teens better manage intense emotions and stresses of everyday life. These evidence-based techniques have been shown to reduce anxiety and depression and improve well-being.
- Mindfulness involves living in the present moment through deep breathing, mindfulness meditation, and grounding techniques. It calms the nervous system and decreases reactivity to stressors. Even brief daily practice can have significant benefits.

- Distress tolerance skills teach riding the waves of difficult emotions instead of making things worse through impulsive actions. Strategies like holding an ice cube or snapping a rubber band can provide a distraction from emotional pain.
- Emotion regulation involves understanding the root causes of emotions to guide actions, not just react on impulse. Tools like journaling, feelings charts, and positive self-talk can help gain insights into emotional patterns.
- Interpersonal effectiveness equips teens to build healthier relationships through assertive communication, active listening, negotiation, and compromise without losing self-respect.
- Taking care of basic physical and mental well-being needs through the PLEASE skill (like proper sleep, nutrition, and exercise) makes managing emotions and stress easier. Self-care is important.
- Communication techniques like DEAR MAN and objectively describing situations can help constructively resolve conflicts and disagreements through validated perspectives and compromise.
- Facing challenges with a positive mindset, resilience, goal setting, and seeking social support leads to overcoming difficulties with confidence and personal growth.

CHAPTER 2

Thriving In Your Environment

"Be happy in the moment, that is enough. Each moment is all we need, not more."

– Mother Teresa

ISN'T IT AMAZING how something as simple as being happy in the moment can make such a big difference? Mother Teresa's words remind us of the power of mindfulness – a practice that has been around for over 2,500 years! It's like a timeless gift that helps us appreciate each moment, right here, right now.

Now, let's talk about something equally important —building harmony and connection with our friends and family. Think of it as creating a beautiful mosaic, where each piece represents a relationship or a cherished moment.

The skills offered through DBT have been tested and proven to be incredibly effective in enhancing these connections. They are helpful tools that help us navigate through the ups and downs of relationships, fostering understanding, empathy, and communication.

Imagine being able to truly cherish the people around you — to understand them better, communicate more effectively, and create a sense of harmony and closeness. It's not just about being physically present; it's about being emotionally connected and present in those moments.

Throughout this chapter, we'll explore practical ways to strengthen these bonds. From active listening and expressing gratitude to setting boundaries and resolving conflicts peacefully, we'll delve into the strategies that can make your relationships flourish.

So, get ready to embark on a journey of connection and appreciation. Together, we'll uncover the secrets to building meaningful relationships and cherishing the beauty of life that surrounds us.

Homefront Hero

Raise your hand if schoolwork ever feels totally overwhelming! Juggling classes, activities, friends, etc., can definitely wear you down. Surveys find stress is the #1 health complaint among teens - but it's within our power to control. Successful folks get where they are by calmly handling stress, not avoiding it. I have insider tips to help you own your education while maintaining balance.

Here are easy science-backed strategies for minimizing stress and maximizing your potential this year:

1. Stay Social

Scheduling time with your crew boosts mental health. Even virtual chats help! Isolation makes stress way worse.

2. Catch Zzzs

7 to 9 hours of sleep per night improves focus and your ability to cope. Invest in cozy sheets for comfy resting.

3. Get Moving

Exercise gets feel-good endorphins flowing to melt stress away. Even a 10-minute walk does the trick.

4. Fuel Right

Healthy food keeps you full and sharp. Good nutrients aid brain function and stress response.

5. Get Organized

A tidy space prevents future anxiety. Organization declutters your mind for better focus.

6. Manage Your Hours

Setting goals gives structure to tackle to-dos. Track tasks digitally to easily see your progress.

7. Ask for Help

Teachers understand student challenges – reach out this week if you need guidance.

8. Schedule 'You' Time

Breaks lift your mood more than hours of zoning out. Plan a self-care pack to enjoy mid-day.

9. Check In Regularly

Notice any changes in how you feel or sleep, so use stress-busters before they get out of hand.

Staying calm and thriving this semester is totally within your control! Own it through simple tweaks.

SMILE BREAK!!!

- For a quick stress reliever, try my favorite trick - laughter! Just 10 minutes of giggling works better than most pills.
- Set a timer for 5 minutes. Watch a funny video, see silly memes, whatever makes you chuckle. Count each giggle, guffaw or belly laugh out loud.
- The louder and less graceful, the better. Feel free to look ridiculous! Laughter boosts mood, lowers stress hormones, and improves health.
- Give it a try now before moving on. Your mind and body will thank you later. Let me know how many laughs you get!

DBT Skills and Stress

We all know stress comes with being a teen - school, friends, family, etc. If left unmanaged, it can really impact your mood and performance. That's where DBT comes in with dope skills to handle tough feelings way better. These strategies have helped tons of people through major challenges. Let's check out some that'll help you own your emotional wellness!

1. Visualization

Picture your chill place in your mind. Feeling the sand and hearing the waves mentally gets you out of stress for real. Studies show it reduces pain and anxiety by up to 25%.

2. Finding Meaning

Even imperfect times can have positives if you look for what you gain. Giving situations purpose through your values lowers cortisol levels by up to 20%.

3. Relaxing Hobbies

Do something that stimulates mind relaxation, like drawing, playing an instrument, or watching TV. Calming activities decrease inflammation and brain threat signals.

4. Prayer

It doesn't matter if praying's not normally your thing. Take a second to ask your higher power, or just yourself, for the strength to get through whatever's bringing you down.

> ### FACT CHECK:
>
> Prayer activates the parasympathetic nervous system to slow heart rate and lower blood pressure, calming the "fight-or-flight" stress response. According to Kahneman's System 2, seeking guidance from yourself utilizes higher-level thinking.
>
> "Kahneman's System 2 refers to conscious, deliberate thinking involving higher-level cognitive functions like reasoning and problem-solving."

5. Staying Positive

Talk to yourself like a friend - with kindness, not criticism. Optimism raises your self-worth better than harsh words.

6. One Thing At A Time

In stress, notice small details instead of everything at once. Forest instead of trees, you know?

7. Take Time For You

Even brief breaks replenish your thinking. Walks or quick games decompress your brain so you can handle life like a champ.

These tools truly improve how you experience pressure. Feeling in control of your emotions through simple changes is dope, right? Now you've got major stress-fighting power on your side.

Responding To Emotion

Feeling all the feels is totally normal as a teen – but letting them control you isn't cool. Researchers say being aware of your internal state helps you stay in control of stress and emotions. Pretty neat, right?

On average, teens experience over 100 emotions daily. While feelings are natural, not managing them right can strain your relationships. But those who understand their moods better get along with friends and teachers' way more.

Try these tips to keep your emotions from sabotaging your life:

1. Notice How You Feel

Simply recognizing how you physically and mentally feel can help calm things down. Saying "I'm stressed" or "My heart's racing" acknowledges what's up internally first.

2. Be Kind to Yourself

When big feelings come, use gentle self-talk like "I've got a lot going on." Treat yourself with care – you're only human!

3. Connect to What Matters

Let your priorities like school or friends guide you, not your feelings alone.

4. Try Calming Tactics

We've all chilled out before – laugh with friends, blast music, breathe. Keep experimenting till you find your stress-free zone.

5. Don't Freak Over Freaking Out

Relax, emotions come and go. Stay flexible instead of pressuring yourself to change how you instantly feel. You've got this!

With practice, it really does get easier to handle whatever moods come your way. Manage your emotions and enjoy a much smoother HS experience!

TRY THIS EMOTIONAL FIRST-AID ROLEPLAY!

Practice cooling heated talks fast with this quick activity:
- Pair up and take turns roleplaying a disagreement, like arguing over who left dishes undone.
- Use the anger interruptions! For example, the listener pauses for 6 seconds before responding, or checks in by asking, "Are you good?"
- Switch roles and try letting the facts do the talking instead of emotions.
- Take turns seeing the bigger picture of why dishes matter and how to find a fair solution.
- Encourage positive vibes by emphasizing cooperation over criticism.

Test out these anger stops in a low-stakes scenario. See how they can transform anger into understanding and productive problem-solving faster than ever! Master these moves and you'll have emotional first aid down pat.

Tolerating Distressful Situations

Nobody likes feeling upset, but life throws challenges. As teens, we deal with so much pressure - classes, friends, family issues, etc. However, research shows that specific "distress tolerance" strategies help you stay calm, even during rough times. Practicing these now makes hardships way easier to handle, both now and later on.

Distress tolerance means being in control of your actions and emotions, even when super stressed. It prevents you from being overwhelmed, so you can properly deal with issues. The techniques are simple but scientifically proven to relax your nervous system and clear your mind.

Here are some techniques I recommend trying when you're stressed:

1. Shift Your Focus

Distract yourself by gaming, creativity, or chilling with pals. Out of sight, out of mind is real.

2. Self-Soothe

Use your senses with scents, tastes, music, etc. to calm down. Treat yourself to whatever relaxes you.

3. I.M.P.R.O.V.E Your Mood

Adjust how you visualize stress, practice control, find purpose, and more with this proven method.

4. Weigh the Pros & Cons

Consider the upside of dealing with feelings versus not when upset. Understanding helps relaxation.

5. TIPP Skills

Switch up your body temperature, move around, breathe, or relax tight spots for quick physiological fixes.

6. Emotions Management Techniques

Keep busy until emotions pass through hobbies, supporting others, and scenery changes.

IMAGERY Imagine yourself dealing with the problem successfully & feeling accomplished when it's over. Visualize yourself in a calm and positive place.

MEANING Find meaning in the current challenge. Ask yourself, What can I learn from this experience? How can I grow from this?

PRAYER This can come in any form that works for you. Prayer can be to the universe, God, or your higher self. Connect, surrender your problems, and ask for guidance.

RELAXATION Due to fight or flight, we tense up in stressful situations. Relax your muscles, practice deep breathing & engage in relaxing activities.

1 THING IN THE MOMENT Stay present, find one thing to do & focus entirely on it. Thinking about the past or future will not help.

VACATION Take a break to do something you enjoy. Call a friend or go for a walk. OR Take a vacation in your mind. Visualize yourself on the beach or going for a long drive.

ENCOURAGEMENT Activate your inner cheerleader. Repeat affirmations like, "I've got this," "I'm strong enough to handle this," "This too shall pass."

TEMPERATURE
Change your body temperature. Splash your face with cold water, hold an ice cube, let car AC blow on your face, take a cold shower

INTENSE EXERCISE
Do intense exercise to match your intense emotion. Sprint to the end of the street, do jumping jacks, push ups, intense dancing

PACED BREATHING
Try Box Breathing: Breathe in for 4 seconds, hold it for 4 seconds, breathe out 4, and hold 4. Start again, and continue until you feel more calm.

PAIRED MUSCLE RELAXATION
Focus on 1 muscle group at a time. Tighten your muscles as much as possible for 5 seconds. Then release & relax. Repeat with other muscle groups.

These strategies really work. Practicing them now boosts your resilience and well-being for life. You've got the power tools to handle any challenge, friend.

Handling Rejections from Peers

Not feeling included by friends totally sucks. But listen up - having close pals isn't everything. Researchers found DBT strategies can seriously help cope with social stress. Just remember - acceptance starts from within, not others' opinions.

Our caveman's brains evolved to want social acceptance. So, rejection feels awful! But using these techniques takes back your power. Stay strong - it gets better.

1. Own It

Admit what happened. Feel your feelings fully, then brush it off.

2. Don't Personalize

Their actions say more about them. Remind yourself their choices don't define your worth.

3. Let It Out

Cry to friends or alone. Emotions need to be felt to heal.

4. Lean on Your Squad

They've got your back to lift you up. Friendship is a two-way street.

5. Focus on Growth

Compare just yourself from yesterday. We all grow at our own pace.

6. Try New Things

Branch out your interests through activities. Potential new friends await!

7. Pamper Yourself

Self-care=happy you. Give yourself love and care.

8. Look on the Bright Side

Rejection happens - you'll get through this stronger.

9. Accept Yourself

Your worth isn't measured by others' opinions. Embrace who you are fully.

10. Quality over Quantity

Having a few close friends is better than feeling unsupported in a crowd.

You've got amazing times ahead. Stay strong and keep practicing these skills - they work!

Now that you understand how you can apply DBT skills let's explore how these skills can further improve your quality of life, leading to greater happiness, fulfillment, and success in various aspects of your life.

Key Takeaways

- Practicing mindfulness and using DBT skills can enhance happiness and improve relationships.
- Nurturing family connections through activities like spending quality time together fosters understanding and empathy.

- Simple actions like encouraging parents to spend time alone, including all family members in conversations, and fostering teamwork can strengthen family bonds.
- To manage school stress, focus on social interactions, get enough sleep, exercise, eat well, stay organized, seek help when needed, and take breaks.
- DBT offers effective strategies such as imagery, finding meaning in difficulties, deep breathing, meditation, prayer, focusing on one thing at a time, taking breaks, and positive self-talk.
- Recognize emotions, be kind to yourself, connect to what's important, use chill strategies, and avoid stressing about stress.
- Handle conflicts calmly by responding thoughtfully, pausing for 6 seconds, listening to others, sticking to facts, considering different perspectives, staying positive, and avoiding blame.
- Develop distress tolerance through distraction, self-soothing with senses, using the IMPROVE acronym, weighing pros and cons, using TIPP skills, and engaging in activities.
- Respond positively to rejection by owning it, not taking it personally, expressing emotions, seeking support, trying new things, practicing self-care, staying positive, and valuing quality friendships.

CHAPTER 3

Crafting Your Ideal Life

> *"The key to emotional mastery is not to fight your emotions, but to allow them to flow through you like water."*
>
> **– Mark Manson**

EMOTIONS ARE A natural part of being human. As Mark Manson said, they flow through us like water. For teenagers especially, this can sometimes feel more like a raging rapid!

The hormone and brain changes associated with adolescence mean teens experience emotions more intensely than children or adults. Just thinking about being a teen again makes me empathize — it is a wild rollercoaster of joy, stress, anger, and everything in between.

Studies actually show that the teenage brain is biologically wired to focus more on emotions. This helps you build important social skills as you become more independent. However, it also means you feel ups and downs more powerfully as you figure out who you are.

When emotions run high, it's easy to get swept up in the current. However, self-care is the lifejacket that helps you ride the wave instead of drowning in it. Making time to recharge is so important for your well-being.

Did you know 75% of teens report feeling high levels of stress? Yet only 17% feel they are managing it very well. Prioritizing yourself might not always seem exciting. But taking care of your mental and physical health lays the groundwork for everything – school, friendships, hobbies, and your future.

In the following pages, we'll explore simple, yet powerful self-care strategies customized for busy teenagers like you. From managing stress to fueling your body right, these tips will help keep your head above the emotional rapids so you can truly enjoy your teenage adventure!

Self-Care Superstar

I know routines sound kinda boring but hear me out. Pro athletes, designers, and big shots all swear by them! From basketball player Michael Jordan to fashion designer Calvin Klein. Shocking right?

> *"We are what we repeatedly do. Excellence is a habit, not an act."*
>
> **- Aristotle**

Having rituals is like building good habits. You can start small, like journaling or meditation daily. Over time, these habits will stick, and you can do more without stressing as hard.

When I was in high school, routines were the last thing I wanted. But making your own schedule with activities you enjoy means being in control instead of constantly reacting to what life throws at you.

In the next sections, I'll share some routine tips tailored just for us crazy-busy high schoolers. You can try the ones that appeal most to you to start developing good habits. The best part is you can tweak until you find what truly works magic for your unique lifestyle. Who knows, maybe you'll become a routine rockstar too!

Morning Rituals to Level Up Your Day

1. Rise and Shine Early

I know it's tempting to snooze, but waking up at the same time means more hours to crush your goals. Bonus: You'll feel less rushed getting ready for school.

2. Make Your Bed

It takes about 2 minutes tops, but seeing your neat bed gives you a nice sense of accomplishment to kick things off.

3. Affirm Your Awesomeness

Say nice things about yourself in the mirror to hype yourself up, like, "I'm gonna rock this test today!" Self-love is key.

4. Stretch It Out

MOTIVATION STATION

Turn your space into a positive affirmation power center! Cut out inspirational phrases and pictures from magazines to decorate your mirror, desk, or locker.

Need mantras? Try:

- "I am brave, strong, and beautiful"
- "Today is going to be awesome!"
- "The future is mine"
- "I've got this in the bag!"

Make it bright with color markers and stickers too. Change up the notes weekly for a fresh dose of encouragement. Who knows, you might start believing them for real!

It's your morning motivation makeover. Feel free to personalize it with inside jokes or sayings that make you smile. Soon your vibe will be totally lit!

Do a few yoga moves or go for a jog - exercise wakes your brain up, and you'll feel more energetic all day.

5. Eat a Nutritious Breakfast

Fuel up on protein, fruits, and grains. It'll stop you from crashing later and keep you learning at max power.

6. Hydrate!

Keeping water next to your bed means you'll start hydrating. Bonus points if you add fruit for flavor.

7. Take an Icy Shower

The cold wake-up gives you an adrenaline rush, and you're ready to face anything! It might be an acquired taste, but it feels great.

Tweaking small habits each day means continuous improvement. I hope some of these helps you start strong! Let me know your favorites.

Hey everyone, now that we've covered some awesome morning routines to jumpstart your day, let's talk about equally important evening rituals to wind down and prep for tomorrow!

Evening Routines to Set Yourself Up for Success

When the day is done, it's time to relax your brain and recharge. These end-of-day habits will help you feel less stressed and more ready to rock the next day.

1. Unplug from Screens

We all know how easy it is to scroll mindlessly on your phone in bed. But the blue light doesn't relax your brain at all. Try to power down devices at least 30 minutes before bedtime, so you actually feel tired. You can read a book or magazine instead.

2. Journal About Your Day

Jotting down three fun things that happened or how you're feeling is a quick mental cleanse. Seeing your thoughts on paper can help you process emotions and goals. Bonus: it's a cool way to look back years later!

3. Stretch Your Muscles

Moving your body, even for 5-10 minutes, helps you wind down and sleep better. Rolling your neck, touching your toes, or following a quick yoga video on YouTube feels amazing after sitting all day.

4. Meditate

Downloading a meditation app is a calming way to chill your thoughts. Start with just five minutes if you're new to it. The relaxation you feel after is so worth it.

5. Plan Your Next Day

Write a quick to-do list or schedule for tomorrow morning so you go to bed feeling prepared. Bonus points if you lay out your clothes or pack your bag tonight, too!

6. Read Something Non-Screen

Curl up with a book, magazine, or comic rather than social media right before bed. The focused attention helps satisfy your brain in a relaxing way.

7. Have a Bedtime Routine

Whether it's brushing your teeth, skincare, or lighting candles – doing the same soothing activities signals to your body that it's time to rest up for tomorrow. Consistency is key here.

Creating reliable morning and evening routines gives structure to your day without stressing you out. I hope these ideas spark some habits that allow you to feel prepared and recharged each day.

Constant Reflection and Self-Discovery

We all spend tons of time with ourselves, but how well do you really understand who you are? Looking inward isn't always easy, but it's important. Studies show most people aren't that self-aware, though. Only about 10 to 15% people have strong introspection skills.

Examining your feelings and behaviors without judging makes you see your influences, drives, and impulses more clearly. Understanding yourself makes living your best life way more possible.

What is Self-Reflection?

Self-reflection means deeply thinking about who you are, how you feel, and why you act a certain way. It's hitting pause on life to look back at how you reacted to situations without rushing. This gives you insight into your personality and why you do what you do.

While unraveling yourself takes effort, it's so worth it. Getting to know you better helps you succeed personally and socially. The journey inside is lifelong, so start reflecting today!

The best way to reflect is setting aside chill time daily. Get comfy and let your mind wander through feelings and interactions without criticism. Regular self-reflection is key to growth, I promise. You might surprise yourself with how much you can learn. Staying curious about who you are keeps things interesting.

Cool Ways to Get to Know Yourself Better

Figuring yourself out takes time. Don't stress too much - looking inward should make you feel at peace, not freaked out. Chill if you start overthinking. Self-discovery is about understanding who you are, not beating yourself up.

Incorporate self-reflection into your routine. Try doing it when you first wake up or right before bed - when it's quiet. Stick to doing it at the same time each day so it becomes a habit. You won't learn as much if you don't do it regularly.

Here are some laidback methods to try:

1. What Do You Wanna Know?

Think about what questions you want to ask yourself, like "What makes me happy?" or "What went well this week?" Having questions will help guide your thinking.

2. Count Your Blessings

Sit back and list what you're grateful for, big or small. Start with three nice things from your day, then think bigger, like this week or year. Appreciating life can lift your mood.

3. Zen Out

Meditation takes practice but calms your mind. Breathe deep and notice what pops into your head. Patterns may show you what's really up.

4. Map Out Your Goals

Jot down what you want to accomplish and use it to check in on yourself. Are you making progress? Is something holding you back? Figuring that out can help you level up.

5. Put Pen to Paper

Writing your thoughts in a journal processes them and lets you look back later to see how far you've come.

6. Talk to Yourself

Saying thoughts aloud can give you a fresh perspective. It also helps organize what you want to tell others.

7. Chill in Nature

Spending time outside resets stress and lets you focus. Leave distractions at home.

Hope this gives you some chill ways to discover who you're becoming. Let me know if any methods work for you!

<u>BREAK TIME!!</u>

Need a break from the stress? Tired of the same old routines? Try these fun self-reflection activities perfect for when you want to unwind and feel inspired.

- *Smile Squad* - Take a boomerang or short video of you and your squad cracking up.
- *Compliment Attack* - Leave positive notes for your friends in their lunch boxes, lockers, or desks.
- *Random Acts* - Surprise someone with their favorite snack, song, or emoji just because.
- *Friends from Afar* - DM or tweet at friends you haven't talked to in a while.
- *Outta the Comfort Zone* - Try a new sport, or hobby or sit with a different group at lunch.
- *Gratitude Gallery* - Decorate your room or locker with pics of things/people you appreciate.
- *Dream Board Bonanza* - Make a vision board on Pinterest full of your future goals.
- *Memories Galore* - Look through old texts, photos, and posts from fun times.
- *Shoutouts* - Write appreciative social media posts about peers who lift you up.
- *Selfie Station* - Snap colorful, creative, or funny selfies capturing your mood ASAP.

Post these pics on your Close Friends story and don't forget to like other people's too! Having activities, you find fun and engaging can help you feel good while also learning more about yourself.

Breaking Down Big Goals Into Intentional Ones

We all love a good to-do list, but having too many loose goals can lead you nowhere fast. It's better to focus your energy on a few key targets that really fire you up.

But how do you pick the right ones? Well, it's easy to get distracted chasing what others want instead of your own dreams. Don't fall for the hype - figure out what truly inspires YOU.

A sure sign goals aren't right? If they keep changing, it means they don't align with your core self. Goals set just because "that's what you should do" won't light your soul on fire.

This is where finding your why comes in. Getting clear on your purpose and values helps you zero in on meaningful goals that energize you to succeed.

Rather than a messy list, break big plans into clear steps. This gives you a road map to follow at your own pace. Don't stress if detours happen - as long as you're pursuing what's important TO YOU, you're good.

The bottom line? Prioritize goals rooted in self-awareness over impressing others. Discover your way to reach your full potential!

QUEST FOR PURPOSE:

So how do you separate the fleeting whims from the wishes that will bring you lasting fulfillment? It's time to get real with yourself through some crucial soul-searching.

Ask these tough questions that'll help you cut through the noise of outside influence.

- Where do you see yourself in a year?
- What are your priorities right now?
- Are you passionate about these goals?
- How will achieving them make you feel?
- Why are these goals important?
- Will they still matter later on?

So, forget distraction and hype - listen to your heart. Discover your purpose and watch your dreams transform from hazy hopes to inevitable realities.

Setting Goals That Stick

A lot of us are all talk when it comes to making plans for the future. But if you wanna achieve something amazing, listen up. Here are some key things to keep in mind when setting goals:

1. Write It Out

Putting pen to paper makes goals way more real. Your thoughts become intentions!

2. Break It Down

Don't just say, "I wanna be rich." Break big dreams into small, weekly steps to stay motivated.

3. Get An Accountability Buddy

Find someone who'll check on your progress to keep you focused.

4. Be Specific

Vague goals like "learn guitar" don't help much. Detail what you'll achieve by when.

5. Set Deadlines

Don't just "aim to finish by summer." Put dates in your calendar so you can deliver.

6. Reward Yourself

Treat yourself when you hit little milestones to celebrate accomplishments.

Setting clear intentions with structure and a team behind you is key to making your goals a reality. Don't just talk about change - act!

Actionable Formulation

It's not enough to just dream about the future - you gotta take action! An important part of goal setting is turning plans into an actual game plan. Here's how to craft goals that motivate you to move:

Make an Action Plan

An action plan is like a checklist that helps you organize and prioritize your objectives. Break big dreams down into smaller steps you can tackle week by week.

Why It Helps:

- Keeps you focused on the progress
- Shows what needs doing and when
- Gives directions if you get lost or stuck

What Goes In It:

- Detailed tasks required for the goal
- Deadlines for each piece
- Resources/help needed
- Potential roadblocks

Use Templates

Templates online make planning a breeze. Just fill in the blanks for your specific goal.

Stay on Track

Review your plan regularly to stay motivated. Cross off completed steps and adjust due dates if needed.

Having a concrete plan of attack transforms goals from fuzzy notions into achievable realities. With the right strategy, you'll stay determined to see your vision through to the end.

Taking Action to Reach Your Goals

Creating an action plan is an important part of setting yourself up for success. It helps transform vague goals into concrete objectives that you can actively work toward. Here are the key steps to develop a thorough action plan:

1. Start With SMART Goals

Be specific, measurable, achievable, relevant, and time-based. For example, instead of "get in shape," set a goal to "lose 10 pounds in 3 months."

S	**Specific**	Make your goal specific and narrow for more effective planning
M	**Measurable**	Make sure your goal and progress are measurable
A	**Achievable**	Make sure you can reasonably accomplish your goal within a certain time frame
R	**Relevant**	Your goal should align with your values and long-term objectives
T	**Time-based**	Set a realistic but ambitious end date to clarify task prioritization and increase motivation

2. Break It Down

Once you have your overall goals, break them down into small, manageable tasks. For example, if your goal is to start a business, you may have tasks like "research business ideas" or "create a marketing plan."

3. Assign Deadlines

Give each task a target date for completion. Use a calendar to assign deadlines for the week, month, or project overall. This keeps you accountable and on track.

4. Identify Resources Needed

For each task, list any resources like money, materials, or help required. This prepares you for potential obstacles.

5. Assign Responsibilities

If working with others, allocate who is responsible for what. Clearly define roles and expectations.

6. Monitor Your Progress

Check-in regularly and note task progress. Mark completed action items off your list as a reward. Adjust deadlines if needed as your project evolves.

7. Review and Celebrate

Periodically review your plan to see what's working and what needs improvement. Celebrate wins to stay motivated toward your end goal. With the right action plan, our goals are 100% achievable!
Tracking And Celebrating Milestones

REMEMBER!!

- Use templates to stay organized
- Adjust dates if life happens but don't bail on your vision
- Celebrate wins to stay amped

Tracking And Celebrating Milestones

Want some motivation to achieve your goals? Celebrating little wins along the way is key. It keeps you fired up to reach the next level.

Did you know that rewarding your progress boosts happiness? When you crush small milestones, your brain releases dopamine - the feel-good chemical. Celebrations remind you how far you've come, increasing your determination to push onward.

Don't just focus on the final result. Track your performance and shout out achievements, no matter how small. Some ways to do this:

- Mark completed tasks on your action plan with a gold star.
- Take selfies flexing new muscles as you get fitter.
- Update friends and family with what you accomplished.

Have success parties your way - blast your jam while doing a victory dance, treat yourself to snacks, or kick back to refuel.

Doesn't that statement make you want to get hyped up? By recognizing progress frequently, you feed motivation to reach your full potential. Don't sleep on celebrating—it's a key to transforming goals into reality.

FACT!!

Only 8% of New Year's resolutions are successful long-term. But celebrating baby steps at least doubles your chances of long-run success!

Awesome Ways to Celebrate Reaching Your Goals

Scoring a win is super important, so make sure you whoop it up when hitting a milestone. Celebrations keep your motivation flowing strong as you pursue the next level. Here are some fun ideas to get hyped up about your progress:

1. Treat Yourself

Reward all your hard work however you like —whether it's your favorite snack, a spa day, or awesome new gear for your hobby.

2. Party with Your Squad

Share the love by throwing a kickback with friends and family who rooted for you.

3. Start New Traditions

Come up with signature ways to mark occasions, like lighting an accomplishment candle or high-fiving your favorite tree in the park.

4. Write Yourself a Note

Pen an encouraging letter recognizing everything you overcame to get here.

5. Create a Vision Board

Feast your eyes on the imagery of what's coming next as you visualize even bigger wins.

However, you get your props; celebrating benchmarks feels amazing. It motivates you to keep climbing while letting your dedication shine through.

Celebrating isn't just about feeling accomplished - it reminds you of the effort put in and reasons to keep grinding! Treat yourself to staying dedicated to your goals. You deserve it!

Staying Pumped After Hitting A Goal

Snagging a huge win is so dope, but keeping up your grind afterward takes work too. Here are some ways to keep the flames lit:

1. Keep the Momentum

Toppling obstacles to succeed built sweet skills - use them to blast off toward the next level!

2. Set New Objectives

Celebrate achievements, then whip out new badass challenges to take on.

3. Chill for a Sec

Doing major things can drain you - recharge so you come back stronger. Just don't Netflix for too long!

4. Track Your Triumphs

Remembering how far you've come will fuel your fire when the drive starts drifting.

5. Hype Small Successes Too

Mini wins keep the positive vibes flowing between massive milestones.

So, throw awesome parties to honor reaching your goals, then stay lit through the challenges ahead. Your next epic wins await if you keep that motivation game tight!

Building a Solid Squad at Home

Staying tight with your crew is essential, but sometimes, real life can put stress on your family bonds. From busy schedules to constant competition, it's easy for relationships at home to start feeling strained. But relaxing connections with siblings and parents should be a top priority. Because let's be real - who's always got your back no matter what? FAMILY.

If hanging with your crew is starting to feel like a chore, it may be time to switch up your strategy. Lucky for you, I've got 10 proven techniques to bring more harmony into your home base. From finding low-key activities everyone enjoys to managing stress together, these tips will make your squad tighter than ever. So, say goodbye to drama and hello to a quality family time where everyone feels appreciated. It's time to strengthen those core relationships and remember - you're all on the same team. Let's get to strengthening that home front!

1. Chill Communication

Small talk stress? Switch it up with smiles. Watch your tone and think before speaking - respect goes a long way.

2. Appreciate Your Tribe

Make each family member feel welcomed with compliments. Acknowledge their good traits and make them feel special. Celebrate what makes each family member unique.

3. Custom Cozy Time

Low-key activities you all enjoy are the most relaxing. Do casual activities together without competition, stealing the fun. Stress Less, Laugh More. Find your favorite feel-good fixes as a squad.

4. Plan and Come Together

Get on the same page about your week ahead. Chat about your weeks on Sundays so you're all on the same page.

5. Take Time for Yourself Too

Schedule relaxing solo time to avoid stress maxing you out. "Say No and Say Yes to You," know it's okay to set limits for downtime. Set 10 minutes just for you solo time.

6. Get Moving Outdoors

Nature is soothing - escape your devices for fresh air together. The outdoors is perfect for recharging your mind and soul.

7. Think Positively

Let go of rude attitudes and look for the bright side of people instead. Look for the bright side in each other.

Your home is your sanctuary. Filling it with warmth, respect, and good vibes makes enjoying family that much sweeter. Minor changes can seriously boost harmony.

SELF-CARE STAR CHALLENGE

You've learned some awesome tips to nourish your mind, body, and relationships. Now it's time to try them out!

For the next week, commit to doing one new self-care activity each day. Maybe you meditate on Monday, go for a nature walk on Wednesday, and have a family game night on Friday. Be creative - find low-key ways that work for you.

At the end of the week, check in with how you're feeling. Are you better able to manage stress? Do you feel more connected to friends and family? Keep up the healthy habits that are working and don't be afraid to tweak things that aren't clicking for you.

You got this! Taking care of yourself takes effort but pays off big time. Share your favorite activities on social media with the hashtag **#SelfCareStar.** Stay glowing, friends!

You've Come a Long Way!

Congrats - by taking the steps in this chapter to set goals, prioritize self-care, and strengthen important bonds, you're well on your way to living your best life. Developing healthy habits and maintaining strong relationships is an ongoing journey, so keep reflecting and adapting your strategies as you grow.

Now that you have tools to care for your well-being, your relationships will benefit too. In the next chapter, we'll discuss how cultivating self-care and harmony at home can positively influence your relationships with friends, and mentors, and contribute to creating a kinder community. But for now, be proud of the skills you've learned and all you've achieved so far. Keep shining bright - you've got this! I'm excited to see where your journey leads you next.

Key Takeaways

- Understand that emotions are natural, especially during adolescence, and learn to flow with them instead of resisting.
- Prioritize self-care to manage stress and maintain well-being, which lays the foundation for success in various aspects of life.
- Establish morning routines to boost productivity, set a positive tone for the day, and build healthy habits effortlessly.
- Wind down with evening rituals that promote relaxation, reflection, and preparation for the next day.
- Practice self-reflection to gain clarity on your thoughts, feelings, and behaviors, leading to better self-awareness and personal growth.
- Set meaningful, specific, achievable, and time-bound goals aligned with your values and purpose to stay motivated and focused.
- Create actionable plans with clear steps, deadlines, and accountability to turn goals into tangible accomplishments.
- Celebrate milestones along the way to maintain motivation and track progress effectively.
- Strengthen relationships with family through effective communication, mutual appreciation, shared activities, and positive attitudes.

CHAPTER 4

Mastering Your Relationships

> *"We can improve our relationships with others by leaps and bounds if we become encouragers instead of critics."*
>
> **– Joyce Meyer**

HAVE YOU EVER felt misunderstood or like your relationships could use a boost? The truth is that communication is key to forming strong bonds - but it's not always easy. With some self-awareness and new techniques, you can level up how you connect with others.

Experts estimate that over 70% of conflicts stem from crossed signals or lack of understanding between people. When our emotions run high, it's easy to react instead of responding thoughtfully. But learning to recognize how you feel in the moment is a game-changer. Studies show that students with high emotional intelligence have lower stress levels and get along better with peers.

In this chapter, we'll explore simple strategies to expand your "emotional vocabulary" so you can name feelings as they come up. Once you can identify triggers, you gain power over your reactions. Plus, sharing vulnerability with care and honesty builds trust. We'll also cover active listening to understand other people's views better.

By tapping into your emotional skills and focusing on compassion over criticism, your relationships have room to grow like never before. Are you ready to level up how you influence those around you? Let's learn ways to empower yourself and others through communication. The bridges we build start from within.

Communication Champion

Ever feel like your emotions can be a mess when interacting with others? That's where emotional intelligence (EQ) comes in. EQ is understanding and handling feelings in a chill way, as well as understanding the emotions of others.

It involves self-awareness, self-control, and social skills - super important for getting along with others. You might be book-smart, but EQ helps you succeed socially by connecting with people and navigating conflicts.

It's been shown that high EQ folks tend to be happier and less stressed, too. The good news is you can work these muscles through practices like naming your vibes, active listening and knowing your triggers.

Once you recognize why certain things get you riled up, you have power overreacting versus responding thoughtfully. I've been practicing EQ, and it's already improving my daily social interactions.

Why don't you guys give emotional intelligence a try, too? Improving these skills can boost your friendships and relationships. Let me break down some key EQ tactics:

Emotional intelligence:
the 4 components

Self-awareness

Self-regulation

Social awareness

Relationship management

1. Self-Awareness

Knowing what pushes your buttons is key. To develop self-awareness, pay attention to how you react to different situations. Understanding your feelings will help you stay in control of them.

2. Self-Control

Once you're aware of your emotions, it's about keeping cool when stressed. Learning to wait to express yourself is better than just reacting without thinking.

5 COMPONENTS OF EMOTIONAL INTELLIGENCE
How to Increase EQ In Your Life and Workplace

1	2	3	4	5
SELF-AWARENESS	SELF-REGULATION	MOTIVATION	EMPATHY	SOCIAL SKILLS
Recognizing and understanding one's own emotions, strengths, weaknesses, and triggers.	Managing and controlling emotional reactions to situations, rather than being controlled by them.	(Intrinsic & Extrinsic) Channeling emotions to set and achieve meaningful goals, even in the face of challenges.	Sensing and understanding the emotions of others and showing compassion and consideration.	Navigating social interactions, building rapport, and effectively communicating with others.

3. Social Skills

Being a good conversationalist means actively listening and connecting with people on a real level. Work on communication skills to strengthen your bonds.

4. Empathy

Seeing outside your own perspective takes empathy. Putting yourself in someone else's shoes helps you understand them better so you can all get along.

5. Motivation

Find passion in stuff you're into for its own sake, not just likes or cash. Internal drive makes you an inspiration to others, too.

GIVE YOUR EQ A BOOST WITH THIS QUICK CHALLENGE!

When was the last time you stopped to tune into your own emotions? Need a refresher on emotional awareness?

Try this 5-minute exercise now:

- Take a few deep breaths and notice how your body physically feels. Are you relaxed or tense? Next, think of the last interaction you had. How did it make you feel below the surface - happy, annoyed, left out? No judgment - name the emotion accurately.
- Once you've identified one feeling, think back to other recent experiences and try labeling another emotion. The more you practice this, the better you'll get at picking up on emotional cues from yourself and others.
- Challenge your friends to a feelings face-off too! Share one emotion each and try to one-up each other with specific scenarios that illustrate it even more. Not only is this a fun game, but flexing emotional muscles regularly is proven to boost empathy over time.

Give your self-awareness superpowers a workout. The difference emotional intelligence can make will have you wanting more strategies in no time!

DBT and Healthy Communication Skills

Have you ever found yourself in a situation where your relationships with your friends or loved ones become extra dramatic? Are you constantly arguing over little stuff or feeling guilty just for speaking up? I used to deal with that all the time until I learned some next-level communication skills, all thanks to DBT.

DBT is full of strategies for handling relationships better. Just tweaking how you get your point across can totally minimize misunderstandings. One essential part of DBT is learning interpersonal effectiveness. The idea is to balance what you want with being respectful at the same time.

Can you imagine how much smoother your interactions would go if you had strategies for active listening, compromise, and expressing feelings constructively?

A study found that students who took DBT communication skills training reported 30% fewer conflicts at home within just three months! These tools aren't just for serious problems; they make day-to-day conversations smoother.

Want to strengthen your social game and really level up your connection with people? It starts with integrating a few key DBT practices. I'll break down some specific strategies you can try that will help you build stronger relationships before you know it. Sound interesting? Keep reading to activate your communication superpowers!

DEAR MAN
for getting what you want

describe
the situation using facts

express
feelings and opinions

assert
by asking or saying no

reinforce
ahead of time by
explaining consequences

mindful
keep your focus

appear confident
by voice tone and manner

negotiate
and be willing to give to get

GIVE
for keeping relationship

gentle
no attacks, threats,
or judgements

interested
listen to the other person

validate
acknowledge person's feelings,
wants difficulties, and opinions

easy manner
use humor, smile, ease

FAST
for keeping self-respect

fair
to self and others

aplogies
NONE of that

stick to values
don't sell out and be clear

truthful
don't lie, act helpless,
or exaggerate

1. DEAR MAN to the Rescue

This skill is clutch for clearly asking for what you need while still honoring other people. Just follow the acronym:

D - Describe what you specifically want using facts, not assumptions.

E - Express how you truly feel about the situation in "I" statements instead of blaming.

A - Assert yourself clearly by plainly stating your request or boundary.

R – Reinforce by explaining the positive results of them agreeing to get them on your side.

M – Be mindful, stay focused on the topic if they get defensive, and repeat your point calmly.

A - Appear confident by maintaining eye contact and believing you deserve this.

N - Be willing to negotiate some middle ground so it works for everyone.

2. GIVE Feelings

Use GIVE to show respect to others during talks:

G - Gently listen actively and validate what they say to show you care.

I - Interested in their viewpoint by actively listening, nodding, making eye contact, and reflecting.

V - Validate their thoughts and feelings by reflecting without repeating or checking facts.

E - Easy manner—aware of body language, tone, volume, speed of voice, smiling.

3. FAST for Self-Respect

Using FAST helps communicate respect for yourself:

F - Fair interpretations and aim for mutually beneficial solutions.

A - Apologize specifically, not generally, to avoid contradicting values.

S - Stick to your personal values and don't give them up to please others.

T - Talk truthfully with authenticity and honesty.

If you want to up your social game overnight, try these communication techniques next time issues arise. The difference could surprise you!

DBT and Resolving Conflicts

Picture this: You're in a fight with your bestie that's quickly spiraling out of control. Harsh words are flying, and that sinking feeling of regret starts to set in.

Does this sound familiar? Well, if arguments regularly leave you more frustrated than before, you're not alone. Our brains are programmed to see conflicts as threats, which just makes things worse.

When tensions rise, it's easy to shift into an "emotional mind," where we can only react aggressively or defensively. However, DBT teaches other strategies for switching to a "wise mind" that can minimize the drama. A wise mind is all about cooling off long enough to understand different points of view with empathy instead of just our own feelings.

Did you know that taking a few deep breaths before responding can create clear space to think? Using "I statements" to share how YOU feel takes the blame off others, so they'll actually listen. Truly hearing out what someone else needs and digging to find the real issues keeps conversations constructive instead of in angry circles.

Figuring out compromises you both feel fine with is key, too, since relationships are a two-way street. It takes practice, but just trying DBT's wise mind techniques on the next argument could already be a game-changer. Ready to level up how you work through problems with people you care about? Let's check out some specific tips;

1. See Both Sides

Taking a second to understand where the other person is coming from can truly go a long way. Reflecting on what they said shows you're listening without thinking of your perspective.

2. Broken Record

This one's key if your point won't land. Keep politely repeating your one main message instead of explaining more and giving the other ammo to debate you. Stick to "I feel X," not "because of Y."

3. Get To The Root

If things are just bumping heads, digging deeper with questions like "What exactly about this bugs you?" can uncover the real issues buried under arguing.

4. Find The Middle

Instead of seeing it as all or nothing, try agreeing on one small part as common ground to build on. Ignore extremes and focus on compromise.

5. Press Pause

If the convo's getting heated, it's all right to say, "Let me think on this a bit calmly." Distance gives space to calm down so you can reply thoughtfully versus just in the moment.

6. THINK It Through

Stepping into someone else's shoes can totally change how you react. THINKing things through keeps debates light instead of just bouncing accusations. It gets you closer to truly understanding different views.

T - Think from their perspective. How are they taking it?

H - Have empathy. What might they be feeling angry, sad, or stressed?

I - Interpret positively. What good reason could there be for their actions?

N - Notice efforts. How have they tried to improve or care? We are all struggling.

K - Use kindness. Treat them how you wanna be treated during talks.

So next time tensions rise, try flexing your THINK skill!

Feel understood, stand your ground politely, and solve real problems - those are just a few of the smart ways DBT can next-level your conflict skills overnight.

Managing Familial Relationships

Ever feel like fighting with your family is constantly bringing you down? Dealing with loved ones can be so stressful. Studies show over 60% of teens argue with their parents at least once a week! 80% of us feel crappy for hours after.

But there are dope skills to keep the peace at home without giving up what you need. Most arguments aren't because we hate each other - it's from little misunderstandings blowing up.

Using a few communication tools can transform tense moments before they explode. Like really listening to what people mean below their words to understand feelings. Discussing issues calmly while seeing all sides helps everyone feel heard.

Crazy as it seems, asking how you can support others (not just vent about yourself) can instantly ease drama. Extra kindness benefits us all, right? Improving dynamics through respect makes the family happier, less anxious, and better at working as a team instead of fighting solo.

So next time, debates start brewing, so breathe and try emotional intelligence hacks. I promise it beats constant aggravation any day. Now, how can we achieve that? Keep reading for useful home harmony tips:

1. Radical Listening

Really focus on what the other person is saying without getting distracted. Ask clarifying questions if needed. For example, "What exactly about that situation made you feel frustrated?" Being an active listener shows you care.

2. Stay Cool-Headed

If you start getting riled up, take five slow, deep breaths to calm your nerves. Going for a walk together can also help! Discuss issues while keeping a level, relaxed tone instead of yelling to find solutions, not place blame.

Try these quick strategies to strengthen family bonds:

- *Family Fortune:* Leave kind notes/treats around the house daily.
- *Game Night Guru:* Play non-competitive games 1 night a week.
- *Nature's Nosh:* Pack a nature picnic together once a month.
- *The 10-Minute Massage:* Give quick shoulder rubs to relieve stress.
- *Pep Talks For All:* Compliment 3 things each person did that day.
- Weekend Warriors: Try a new activity together on weekends.
- *Appreciate It Squares:* Write what you love on post its for each other.
- *Tea Time Truce:* Share gratitude over a daily drink together.
- *Sunday Funday:* Go to a museum, hike, or explore your city.
- *Calming Corner:* Designate a quiet spot for alone time.

3. Compromise Squad

Brainstorm options where you both get some of what you want, like dividing chore times fairly. Playing a friendly game together after debates also improves moods. A little cooperation goes a long way.

4. Ask How You Can Help

Ask specific questions like "Is there any way I can lighten your load this week?" Offering a shoulder, cooking a meal, or giving space shows support. Trade-off: Who does the listening/advising, too?

5. Use Kind Words

Leave sweet notes of thanks around the house. Do random acts like hugs, high-fives, or bringing water when someone's stressed. Compliment three things they did that day. Simple gestures go far!

6. Own Your Feelings

When an issue arises, write down thoughts individually, then peacefully discuss them. Drawing how an event made you feel can also get emotions out constructively.

7. Take Breathers

If a discussion starts getting too heated, call for a 10-minute "pause." Go do separate activities you enjoy, and then revisit problem-solving with fresh minds.

THE FAMILY FEEDBACK RELAY !!

Want to level up your fam skills?

Try this fun listening challenge:

Split into pairs and set a timer for 5 minutes. Person A shares anything on their mind while Person B listens without interrupting, just nodding along. Then the timer goes off and Person B must restate what Person A said using their own words. Take turns!

- After, come back together. Discuss things like:
- What was easy/hard about listening deeply?
- How did it feel to have someone restate what you said accurately?
- What can we work on as a family to strengthen our listening?

With practice, you'll be pros at feeling heard, and in turn, really hearing those you care for. Give the Feedback Relay a try and watch family bonds strengthen before your eyes!

Building Boundaries

We all need basic rules to share how we really feel without worries. That means your space and the freedom to believe what you want without downs.

Your feelings and privacy shouldn't just get walked on, either. Little disagreements can blow up if resentments build. But boundaries aren't selfish - they create trust, so everyone gets heard without harshness.

Figuring out what you truly need may take time, but it saves huge drama down the road. Respecting others' limits strengthens bonds way more than constant fighting ever could.

Whether it's speaking up politely when crossed or just having your room as a no-go zone, boundaries with fam can save headaches. It's about caring for yourself. Let me break down some easy ways to set your boundaries up smoothly:

1. **Figure Out Why** - understand what boundaries make you comfortable.
2. **Start Small** - focus on one or two boundaries at first so the changes feel manageable.
3. **Set Boundaries Early** - lay out what you need from the jump before resentment builds.
4. **Stay Consistent** - sticking to limits reinforces who you are.
5. **Schedule 'You' Time** - carve out solo moments to recharge your way.
6. **Say Something Nice** - politely bring up crossed boundaries.
7. **Do Your Thing** - keep being true to yourself so vibes stay cool.
8. **Love Yourself** - nourish your soul so you believe you're worth protecting.
9. **Go With Your Gut** - trust your instincts; boundaries will keep you happy and healthy.
10. **Check Perspective** - balance structure with going with the flow.

THE BOUNDARY CHECK-IN

Want to level up your boundary-setting skills?

Try this awareness activity:

Set a timer for 10 minutes and jot down answers to these questions:

- What are some ways people have crossed my boundaries lately?
- How did those interactions make me feel physically and emotionally?
- What boundaries do I need to communicate better?
- What examples can I use to help others understand my limits?
- Afterward, pick one boundary you'll give more attention to this week. Then try this:
- Enforce it with a polite phrase like "I'm taking a rest from that topic."
- Notice how sticking to your guns affects your mood and stress levels.

Gaining clarity is the first step toward change. With practice, you'll be a pro at caring for yourself while keeping the peace. Just 10 minutes of self-reflection goes a long way - give it a try!

To chill relationships long-term, remember communication, compromise, kindness, and self-care are keys. Problems come up, so respond, don't react. With practice, these can transform how you influence others for the better!

THE 60-SECOND COMPLIMENT DROP !!

Want to boost your relationship IQ right now?

Try this sneaky social skills challenge:

Set a timer for 1 minute and do your best to give a genuine compliment to every person you make eye contact with. It can be something as simple as "I like your shirt" or "You seem really kind."

After your minute is up, discuss with friends:
- How did it feel to hype others up?
- Did receiving compliments feel good?
- What reactions did people have?

Spreading positivity is proven to improve moods! Try continuing your compliments beyond the timer to really strengthen bonds. A little kindness goes a long way - give the Compliment Drop a whirl today!

Relationships are a two-way street, so focus on balancing what you want while honoring others too. If issues do come up, take a wise-mind approach by cooling off first before problem-solving. With practice, these strategies can transform how you influence those around you for the better. After that, we will see how the DBT skills you have learned so far play a significant role in life-threatening situations in the next chapter. Stay tuned!

Key Takeaways

- Understanding and managing your emotions is crucial for successful relationships. It involves self-awareness, self-control, social skills, empathy, and motivation.

- Active listening, expressing feelings constructively, and using "I statements" can prevent misunderstandings and build trust.
- DBT offers strategies like DEAR MAN (Describe, Express, Assert, Reinforce, Mindful, Appear confident, Negotiate), GIVE (Gently listen, Interested, Validate, Easy manner), and FAST (Fair, Apologize, Stick to values, Truthfully) for healthy communication and resolving conflicts respectfully.
- Seeing both sides, staying calm, finding compromises, and using "I statements" can help manage conflicts effectively.
- Radical listening, staying cool-headed, compromising, offering support, using kind words, and respecting boundaries are key to maintaining peace and harmony within families.
- Setting and maintaining boundaries is essential for self-care and ensuring your needs are met without sacrificing your well-being.

CHAPTER 5

Conquering Your Inner Demons

> *"It's not what happens to you but how you react to it that matters."*
>
> **– Epictetus**

EVER FEEL TOTALLY bummed out? You're not alone - around 5% of people struggle with depression at some point. It can seriously mess with your quality of life by robbing you of all joy and hope.

But there are ways to gain power over sadness and start feeling better. DBT has proven super effective for managing depression symptoms. It teaches techniques for riding ups and downs without letting emotions control you.

The core idea is accepting realities while still working on positive change - way easier said than done. Our inner critics love yelling, "It's not fair!" and refusing to accept what is. But constantly fighting reality only causes stress and stops progress.

DBT teaches it's okay to feel crummy - things are crummy - we just can't wallow forever. Mindfulness helps ride emotional waves, and radical acceptance of what you can't change right now gives strength to start stepping toward better days.

As crazy as it sounds, just being able to surf your feelings without drowning is empowering. DBT supercharged my resilience. Strategies like observing thoughts from a distance instead of getting swept up. Practices like emotional regulation and distress tolerance techniques buy breathing room to take back control.

If depression has you feeling like a prisoner to sadness, DBT might be the key. In the next section, we'll explore strategies you can use now. Level up your mental health with curiosity - you've got this!

Winning The War Against Fear

Ever stressed about tests or talks that keep you up at night? Who doesn't get the jitters sometimes? Well, I'm spilling the secret to how manageable it all becomes once you know these techniques.

DBT is like a superpower for realizing fears aren't that scary - they're normal human things we can overcome. So, if anxiety runs the show too much, it's time to step up as the star of your life story.

I'm talking about maximum confidence, where worries used to stand. No more missed chances due to good old nerves. Ready to claim that boldness? Here are some key strategies:

1. Know Your Feelings

Become aware of exactly what's making your stomach flip. Naming the emotion takes its power away. Remember, feeling afraid doesn't define you - it's temporary.

2. Call Out Anxiety's Lies

Once you pinpoint worries, say why those fears won't happen out loud. Maybe a speech won't be perfect, but people understand slip-ups. Tests rarely go totally wrong since you studied.

3. Face Fears Gradually

DBT's "Opposite Action" takes baby steps out of your comfort zone. If meeting people stresses you, force yourself to say hi to one stranger today. Next time, make it two people. Slowly expand your limits.

Conquering anxiety gets easier with practice. Trust that you've got this! With DBT skills, fears won't hold you back anymore.

WHAT IS OPPOSITE ACTION?

Opposite Action is one of the core DBT skills that can help you gain confidence in facing your fears. It involves willingly doing the opposite of what your fear urges you to do.

For example, if giving a presentation scares you because it makes you anxious to be the center of attention, your fear might urge you to avoid raising your hand or volunteering. With Opposite Action, you would force yourself to take the steps toward doing the very thing you're afraid of.

The goal is to disprove the fear by experiencing the feared situation and realizing it's not actually as dangerous as you built it up to be in your mind. By standing up to fears this way, over time they start to lose their power over you.

Some keys to Opposite Action:

- Start small - Don't try to face your biggest fear yet. Build up to it gradually.
- Be prepared - Have coping tools ready like deep breathing if anxiety hits.
- Stay present - Focus on the task, not scary thoughts. Say a mantra like "I've got this!"
- Reward yourself - Praise increases motivation. Celebrate small wins.
- Keep at it - Fear doesn't melt instantly. Stick with Opposite Action consistently.

Remember - you don't need to conquer anxiety in one try. Each step away from avoidance and toward courage is progress. Don't give up, and before you know it facing fears will feel easy-peasy.

QUICK TIP

Choosing Opposite Action
DBT Skill

Initial Emotion	Urge ✗	Opposite Action ✓	Opposite Emotion
Anger	Yell, Argue, Fight	Whisper, Breathe, Hug	Peaceful, Calm
Sadness	Isolate, Cry, Stay in bed	Connect, Laugh, Get up and out	Engaged, Happy
Frustration	Give up, Move on	Take a break, Try again	Mastery
Unworthy	Self-harm, Destructive behaviors	Self-care, Help others	Worthwhile, Useful
Fear	Avoid	Approach	Confident, Brave

Oasis Mental Health Applications

Remember, anxiety's just in your head - it has zero real impact unless you let it. With DBT tools, remind fear who is boss so you can chase goals worry-free. Life's too exciting to miss out due to natural human emotions. You've got this!

FACE YOUR FEARS IN 5 MINUTES

Set a timer for 5 minutes and do something that makes you the tiniest bit uneasy. Maybe it's:
- Saying hi to someone new
- Sitting in the front row of the classroom
- Trying that food, you've been nervous to taste
- Approaching a club/sport you've wanted to join
- Wearing an outfit you're insecure about

While the timer goes, fully embrace the uncomfortable feelings without resisting them. Take deep breaths and remember - you've got this! Once done, reflect on how you felt during and after facing that small fear. Proud? Relieved it wasn't that scary?

With practice, the intense wave of nerves will fade faster every time. And soon you'll be taking on bigger fears without so much as a sweat. Keep challenging yourself to see just how courageous you are! Feel free to share your experience so we can cheer each other on.

DBT and Anxiety

Whether it's worrying about tests, relationships or daily responsibilities, intense emotions can seriously mess with your mojo. The good news is, DBT was made specifically for getting strong against stress, so it doesn't hijack your happiness.

One key DBT concept is called emotion regulation – basically training your brain to manage feelings in a healthier way. See, when nerves strike, our instincts say to avoid anything stressful or escape the situation, but that just lets anxiety run rampant long term. DBT teaches us how to ride the emotional waves with tools like breathing exercises and muscle relaxation instead of fighting or fleeing.

By slowing down our mind and body when on edge, we gain power over overreactions like panic attacks or constant worry spirals. It's like hitting the pause button so we can think before acting on feelings. Over time, these methods literally change our brain patterns to make anxieties way less intense. Crazy right? Just a few minutes a day practicing coping techniques packs a powerful punch against stress.

Now, obviously, I know it's easier said than done at the moment. But DBT makes conquering nerves feel totally doable through practical strategies you can use anytime, anywhere. Wanna learn my favorite on-the-go methods that have seriously saved my bacon more times than I can count? Just keep reading to level up your cool-under-pressure game and gain full control of your mood.

Whether it's test worries, relationship stress, or daily pressures, anxiety can seriously bring you down. Here are a few of my favorite go-to techniques to calm down when experiencing anxiety:

1. Deep Breathing

Oxygen is like rocket fuel for the soul – just five mindful minutes of big inhales and exhales instantly loosens tense muscles and foggy thoughts.

2. Progressive Muscle Relaxation

Take turns squeezing and then relaxing different muscle groups. Releasing bodily tension trains your body to unwind so anxiety has less grip on your mind. Bonus: It's easy to do lying down.

MUSCLE MELTER CHALLENGE !!

Set a timer for 5 minutes and see how many muscle groups you can relax one by one during that time. Here are the steps:
- Start by squeezing your toes/feet muscles as tightly as you can. Hold for 5 seconds then release, feeling the tension melt away.
- Move up to your calves. Squeeze, hold, release. Really focus on the difference between tight and loose muscles.

Set a timer for 5 minutes and see how many muscle groups you can relax one by one during that time. Here are the steps:
- Start by squeezing your toes/feet muscles as tightly as you can. Hold for 5 seconds then release, feeling the tension melt away.
- Move up to your calves. Squeeze, hold, release. Really focus on the difference between tight and loose muscles.

3. Wise Mind Accepting

Feelings aren't facts. Remind yourself that anxious thoughts don't define reality or your worth. Breathe deeply as you embrace emotions without judgment or over-identifying.

4. Distract & Redirect

Ever notice worries spiral when your brain isn't busy? Shift attention by calling a friend, writing in your journal, or enjoying soothing music/ tunes. Steer those thoughts elsewhere.

5. Opposite Action

If avoidance fuels anxiety, face it with small acts of courage, like greeting that intimidating person or trying something new. See, problems aren't as scary as the "what ifs?"

6. Soothe Your Senses

Calm all five feels through touch, sights, scents, etc. Curl up with your favorite snacks, weighted blanket, or music while recharging. Ooey gooey, mindfulness is like an anxiety vaccine!

With practice, these simple DBT methods build boats of bravery to ride life's uncertainties. You've so got this!

5 SENSES GROCERY BAG

When anxiety has you on edge, immersing your senses in soothing stimuli can help take the edge off until feelings pass. Gather a few items and create a homemade "comfy kit" to carry with you.

Fill a reusable grocery bag or Ziploc with 5 things that stimulate your senses in a calming way:
- Visual - Photo of a calm scene, calming coloring page, etc.
- Auditory - Headphones with a relaxation playlist
- Tactile - Smooth stone, fidget toy, stress ball
- Olfactory - Lavender essential oil, calming lotion sample
- Taste - Hard candy, gum, mint

Grab your bag when tensions rise and take yourself on a mindful sensory journey. Close your eyes, listen to music, feel textures, smell scents, enjoy tastes.

Soothing your senses in this DIY spa bag trains your body to relax instead of reacting strongly to stressful feelings. Keep refining your collection - what calming items will you include?

Maintaining a Positive Lifestyle

It's no secret being a teen is tough. Stress can seriously affect both your mental and physical health if left unchecked. However, practicing positivity has been shown to improve mood and life satisfaction long-term.

That's where maintaining a positive mindset comes in. It means catching your bad thoughts automatically with practice. No one knows mindfulness skills better than DBT experts. Strategies like positive self-talk give you power overreactions in hard times.

Adopting even small habits daily can literally change your brain for the better. Read on for proven tips to make positivity part of your lifestyle:

1. **Get Moving** - Exercise boosts energy and mood. Find activities you enjoy, like walks, dancing, and yoga. Even 30 mins helps.
2. **Laugh Out Loud** - Laughter reduces stress instantly. Watch funny videos with friends or tell jokes as a family.
3. **Power Up** - Teens need 8 to 10 hours of sleep to focus. Unplug before bed and develop a relaxing routine.
4. **Declutter Your Space** – Mess stresses you out subconsciously. Straighten for 30 minutes once a week to clear your mind.
5. **Learn New Things** – Challenge your brain with online classes, hobbies, and apps. Acquiring skills feels great.
6. **Give Back** – Volunteer gigs allow you to focus less on problems and more on others.
7. **Spread Kindness** – Little acts of warmth help others and lift you, too.

Keep practicing positivity, and your outlook will follow suit over time. Look for the bright side – you've got this!

Mood Maven

Have you ever felt like things were just heavy - like the whole world was crashing down around you? I think we've all been there at one point or another. As teens, it can feel like the dark times will last forever, but I'm here to tell you there's always hope, even when you can't see the light.

And now that we are at it, let's talk about light. Not the kind that comes from your phone screen at 2 a.m. (we all know that feeling!), but the positive kind. You know, the kind that makes you feel good and hopeful, even when things seem totally dark.

Here's the thing: Life throws curveballs. Tests, drama with friends, family stuff—it can all feel overwhelming. Sometimes, it's easy to get stuck focusing on the negative, like staring at a blank computer screen when you have a project due. Ugh!

But guess what? There's always light, even when you can't see it. Check out this trippy trick: try reading the word **OPPORTUNITYISNOWHERE** super-fast. What did you see first?

OPPORTUNITY IS NOWHERE, or **OPPORTUNITY IS NOW HERE?** Wild, right?

This shows how our brains can twist things around. We might be looking for problems when there are opportunities hiding in plain sight. That's the kind of light we're gonna talk about here—ways to find the good stuff, even when you're feeling stuck in the dark. So, buckle up, Buttercup! We're about to find your inner light switch and FLIP IT ON!

When life gets you down, these tips can help you find the bright side:

1. Stay Present

It's easy to stress about the past or future, but right now is all you got. Focus on noticing good things happening for you in this very moment.

2. Accept What You Can't Control

Sure, some things just suck. But you always control how you respond - choose to stay chill.

3. Start Small

Rome wasn't built in a day. Baby steps to boost your mood are better than no steps. Every little bit helps!

4. Show Gratitude

Thank the universe each day for even one small thing that makes you smile. Seeing blessings keeps more blessings coming.

THE GRATITUDE SPRINT !!

Set a timer for 3 minutes. How many things can you list that you're grateful for before time runs out? It can be big things or small things - your pet, your friends, your health, seeing the sunshine today. Don't overthink - just write as fast as you can!

At the end, count how many things you came up with. I guarantee focusing on what you appreciate, even for a few short minutes, will have you feeling lighter and more positive. Give it a try - then come back and comment how much better you feel!

5. Embrace Growth

Hard times build character - let struggles make you stronger instead of breaking you down.

6. Fake It 'Til You Make It

Pretending to feel happy can trick your brain into being happy. Smile through the bad days.

You Got This!

PUT A POSITIVE SPIN ON IT

Ever notice how your mindset can completely change how you interpret things? Let's practice putting a positive spin on some typically "negative" situations.

Write down three average days you've had lately. Now reframe each one to focus on something awesome that happened, even if minor.

For example:

- Missed the bus → Got extra time to finish my math homework.
- Forgot my lunch → Got to try a new lunch spot with friends.
- Slept through my alarm → Slept great and felt super rested!

Try to notice even tiny positives. Shifting your mindset doesn't have to be hard - sometimes all it takes is a little word tweak! Comment below to share how you positively reframed your days.

When all seems dark, look closer for moments of light. Your thoughts shape your reality - think good vibes into existence. Keep your head up, dudes - brighter days ahead!

I hope these tips and strategies help you learn to manage your mood and find moments of light, even during tough times. Remember - your mindset affects your entire experience, so focusing on gratitude and positivity is a proven way to stay in a good headspace. If you tried the Gratitude Sprint, let me know how you felt afterward - I'm sure you noticed an instant boost.

Now that you've learned about using DBT skills to navigate mental health challenges, it's important to also discuss how these skills can help in dealing with traumatic experiences and intimate partner violence.

Times of trauma can plunge us into deep darkness, but DBT strategies of mindfulness, distress tolerance, and emotion regulation can act as lifelines to guide us toward healing. In the next chapter, we'll look at practical ways DBT can support survivors of trauma and intimate partner abuse on their journey toward empowerment and peace of mind. Stay tuned to learn more.

Key Takeaways

- It's not what happens to you but how you react to it that matters. This perspective can empower individuals facing difficulties.
- A significant portion of the global population struggles with depression, highlighting the commonality of mental health challenges.
- DBT is an effective tool for managing symptoms of depression and intense emotions.
- DBT emphasizes acceptance of life's realities while working toward positive change, mindfulness, and radical acceptance.
- DBT teaches techniques for managing intense emotions, making decisions mindfully, and developing distress tolerance.
- Learning to ride emotional waves without being overwhelmed can empower individuals and restore hope.
- Strategies like recognizing emotions, challenging irrational fears, and gradually confronting stressors can help overcome anxieties.
- Deep breathing, progressive muscle relaxation, distraction, opposite action, and soothing the senses are practical DBT techniques for managing anxiety.
- Maintaining a positive lifestyle through physical activity, laughter, quality sleep, decluttering, learning, helping others, practicing

kindness, affirmations, gratitude, routine, and stress management contributes to mental and physical well-being.

- Being present, accepting what can't be changed, showing gratitude, embracing growth, and staying optimistic are essential for navigating challenges and finding moments of light even in dark times.

Make a Difference with Your Review
Empowering Teens through DBT Skills

"When we meet real tragedy in life, we can react in two ways - either by losing hope and falling into self-destructive habits or by using the challenge to find our inner strength." - Dalai Lama

People who give without expectation live longer, happier lives and make more money. So, if we've got a shot at that during our time together, darn it, I'm gonna try.

To make that happen, I have a question for you...

Would you help someone you've never met, even if you never got credit for it?

Who is this person, you ask? They are like you — or, at least, like you used to be — less experienced, wanting to make a difference, and needing help but not sure where to look.

Our Mission? is to make DBT Skills accessible to everyone. That's the driving force behind everything I do. And the only way we can achieve that is by reaching out to... well.... everyone!!

This is where **you come in.** We often judge a book by its cover (and its reviews), right? So, here's my ask on behalf of a struggling young mind you've never met:

Please help other TEENS by leaving this book a review.

 Your **GIFT** costs **NO MONEY** and takes less than 60 seconds to make real, but You can change a fellow TEENS **LIFE** forever. Your **Review** could help...

...Help a teen find stability in their friendships and goals.

...Assist a kid in smoothing out family relationships.

...upport a student in managing their feelings and academic stress

...Spark a transformation in a teen's life.

...Make one more dream come true.

To get that **'feel good'** feeling and help this person for real, all you have to do is...and it takes less than 60 seconds...

Leave a Review!

Simply scan the **QR code** below to leave your review:

[https://www.amazon.com/review/review-your-purchases/?asin=BOOKASIN\]

If you feel good about helping an anonymous teen gain **DBT SKILLS,** you are exactly my kind of person. **WELCOME** to the **CLUB. YOU'RE** one of **US.**

I am much more excited to help you achieve the skills needed to navigate the teenage emotional drama smoothly. I can't wait to share with you some fantastic communication strategies and life-changing skills in the UPCOMING chapters. Trust me; you're going to love them!

THANK YOU from the bottom of my heart. Now, back to our regularly scheduled programming.

PS: Did You Know? By providing value to others, you become more valuable to them. If you believe this book benefits someone else, why not pass it along?

 Your biggest fan,

 Emma Davis

81

CHAPTER 6

Rising Above Trauma

"The man who moves a mountain begins by carrying away small stones."

– Confucius

HEY GUYS, HAVE you ever felt totally lost after something really bad happens, like you're stuck underwater and can't find your way to the surface? I've been there, and it's the worst feeling ever. But I learned some powerful coping strategies that gave me back control, and I want to share them with you.

Dealing with trauma is so tough as a teen. Did you know that over 60% of kids face some type of abuse, assault, violence, or other traumatic event before they graduate? The stats are crazy! And I know from experience how easy it is to think things will never get better after something goes wrong.

Thankfully, there are effective ways to process pain without it defining you forever. DBT was life-changing for me. It's about riding emotional waves instead of drowning in them, even when the current feels too strong. By using mindfulness, distress tolerance skills, and other DBT techniques, you gain power over trauma's effects on your thoughts and actions.

DBT teaches you to accept harsh realities while still working toward positive change. Even on your worst days, you have power over how you choose to move forward. So, in this chapter, we'll explore strategies designed, especially for teens dealing with trauma or abuse.

Thriving Survivor

Life's been intense lately, right? It's like the world's always trying to bring you down. As teens, the pressure feels intense. I get it - a lot of you have faced bullying, family issues, abuse, or bigger trauma. It's easy to feel alone and trapped by pain.

But you're not alone - half of teens deal with tough stuff. Psychologists find what doesn't kill us can make us stronger. It's called "post-traumatic growth." Bad experiences help you realize your resilience, open your eyes to new opportunities, and tighten bonds. Sometimes, rock bottom brings clarity.

Growth happens naturally with time, but there are ways to speed it up as teens. Rough experiences shape you - you can use what you learned to help others, too! Turn hurt into something good.

DBT gives tools to accept the past without living there forever. Reclaim power over feelings and next steps.

In this part, we'll talk about channeling darkness into fueling an even better you. Finding purpose and using your story lifts mental toughness.

Ever feel crushed by trauma? With post-traumatic growth, rise above it all. This works - you've got this!

The Elements of Growth

Education

Basically, when shit hits the fan, it can totally mess with what you thought you knew about life. Like if you thought bad things only happened to other people or that nothing could disrupt your normal routine. But traumatic events burst that bubble. So, the first step is understanding that your views may need updating now. This can be uncomfortable and confusing, but it also opens a door to seeing things in a new way.

Managing Emotions

Learning anything new is tough when your feelings are all over the place. To work through trauma, you must start by getting a handle on stuff like anxiety, anger, and guilt. Try focusing on the positives instead of what went wrong. Think about your strengths and what you can do going forward. Things like exercise, deep breathing, and talking it out can help calm the storm inside.

Disclosure

Talking about what happened and how it's impacted you is important for making sense of things. It takes the power away from traumatic memories when you share them with someone who cares. A good listener will ask questions to help you understand your experience better versus just bombarding you. Don't be afraid to open up to someone you trust.

5 MINUTES TO A NEW PERSPECTIVE

Hey guys, want to try an activity that'll help you gain a new perspective on pain?

- Take 5 minutes and free write non-stop about a difficult experience from your past, naming all the emotions you felt during and after. Don't worry about spelling or grammar - just get it all out on paper.

- Once those 5 minutes are up, set a timer for 3 more minutes. This time, read back through what you wrote and circle any lessons you learned, strengths you showed, or insights you gained.

- When the second timer goes off, see how you feel. Does focusing on the positives make that memory or situation feel less heavy? You might be surprised by how much power you can take back just by reframing pain as a teacher.

Give it a shot - it could be the first step toward realizing every storm contains rainbows too. And who knows, you may even find your own path to turning tears into triumphs. You've got this!

Narrative Development

This is when you start crafting a story about how you'll move forward after hardship. It's about embracing the chapters that are done but seeing that your book is still being written. Look at people who faced challenges but came out on top — they're proof that you can reshape your narrative into something meaningful.

Service

Helping others is proven to speed up recovery after traumatic events. Even just small acts of kindness can lift your mood and give you purpose. Don't underestimate how much value you have to offer the world, especially those in similar situations.

So, in summary - educate yourself, manage big feels, open up, rewrite your storyline, and lend a hand. Stay tuned for more on how all this leads to growth areas like personal strength, new possibilities, and appreciation for life.

Now that we have talked about how we can grow through difficult experiences. Let's dive into some steps to take the pain and turn it into something meaningful.

5 Steps to Transform Pain into Purpose

Name It

When something super crappy happens, call it what it is. Whether that's a bad breakup, losing your job, getting hurt, or something else. Saying it out loud helps you deal with the emotions instead of keeping it bottled up inside.

List the Lessons

After naming your pain, write down what you learned from going through it. Maybe you discovered new strengths, learned what really matters to you, or gained a new perspective on life. Getting it down on paper can provide clarity.

Define Your Why

What makes you tick? What are your core values? Take some time to reconnect with your reasons for being - the stuff that fuels your interests and passion. Knowing your why will guide your next steps.

Make Those Lessons Count

Look at the lessons again through a new lens. How can you use what you learned to help yourself or others in a positive way? Your experiences uniquely qualify you to support people facing similar situations.

Let It Go

Certain aspects of pain will always hurt, and time is the only remedy. Try releasing what you can't control from the past so your mental energy is free to focus on the present and future.

At the end of the day, it's not about finding the bright side of trauma or twisting bad things into good. It's about building resilience to keep growing despite life's challenges. Stay strong - you've got this!

Patient's Behavioral Change

Ever feel like emotions have you on a spin cycle with no off switch? Been there too many times myself. Half of us face trauma by 16; however, not everyone gets help processing it.

Luckily, DBT was created just for teens like you. It combines coping skills with a supportive environment. Just having someone understand no judgments makes a huge difference. DBT teaches noticing, labeling, and managing big feelings before they take over.

You guys know I'm all about using struggles as building blocks. DBT gives tools to channel junk into growing more assertive, and happier. I've seen firsthand how well it works.

DBT also helps see challenges as opportunities. Sure, trauma feels defining, but strategies let you choose your story's direction instead. Doesn't that beat being a puppet to emotions?

So, if survival mode has you feeling stuck, level up now. You deserve control over your feelings, not the other way around. Let's do this!

We all know how tough change is once habits are set. I'll break down the important aspects and steps to guide positive change. Let's get started!

The 6 Stages of Change

Precontemplation

I do not see a problem yet or want help. Okay, I just want to absorb positive messages here.

Contemplation

The lightbulb's on, but you're not fully ready. Weigh the pros and cons in your own time.

Preparation

You're all in. Research proven strategies so your plan has legs.

Action

Use learned skills and avoid temptation. Reward small victories on the way up.

Maintenance

Appreciate growth and get creative in preventing backslides.

Relapse

Relapse happens to the best of us. See triggers as lessons and re-strategize your determination.

CYCLE OF CHANGE

Remember! Change is a process. Stay patient with yourself as you level up. You've got this!

WANT TO UPGRADE YOUR HABITS FOR GOOD?

Understand These Key Elements of Change First:
- **Willingness:** How motivated are YOU to improve? Changing for your own reasons will stick much better than doing it for someone else.
- **Benefits:** Take time to visualize all the upsides change will bring. Seeing the wins will fuel you through challenges.
- **Barriers:** List any obstacles currently in your way and brainstorm solutions. Knowledge is power - you've got this!
- **Relapse:** Expect slip-ups, but don't see them as failure. Crash and learn from it. Each time you'll bounce back stronger.

Change is a process that takes patience and understanding these core factors. Invest time in yourself - your future self will thank you. Let's level up!

How to Change Your Behavior

I know changing behaviors can seem impossible some days, but don't hit snooze - there are stealth strategies to level up your life that you may not have known about. From tweaking your nutrition one choice at a time to finding physical activities you're actually excited to do, I'm spilling the deets on low-key ways to transform yourself from the inside out.

Let's break down some key areas where habits need upgrading and strategies proven to work.

Nutrition

Instead of going cold turkey, swap one unhealthy food at a time for healthier choices. Small steps mean changes will stick.

Exercise

Find physical activities you genuinely enjoy - then it won't feel like a chore. Leave the car at home sometimes and take the stairs when possible.

Observe Without Judging

Notice patterns and triggers with kindness, not criticism. This open mindset spots chances for better behaviors.

Check The Facts

Impulses can lie, but facts won't. When urges attack, slow down and objectively examine the likely outcomes of each choice.

Radical Acceptance

We all mess up sometimes - that's human. In DBT, this means accepting where you are without shame so you can focus your energy on growing.

Reduce Reactivity

In tough moments, breathe and remember that strong feelings aren't forever. Pause to pick a response you won't regret when calmer.

Distress Tolerance

Crap happens - it's what we do with it that matters. Learn to survive crises with more "whatever" till you're ready to address root issues.

Sleep

Feel like you're always tired? Maintaining your sleep diary and sticking to a strict bedtime schedule, even on weekends, can level you up to well-rested status.

With practice, these skills strengthen your superpower to observe realistically, think clearly in storms, and choose behaviors that feel good later on.

Keep in mind that Rome wasn't built in a day, and changing habits is a process. Go easy on yourself and celebrate stepping stones — you've totally got this!

Emotional Overwhelm Versus Emotional Numbness

Ever feel like you're on a rollercoaster of emotions one minute and then completely flat-lined the next? Yeah, us, too. Being a teenager is tough – tons of pressure, social drama, and the ever-present feeling of the world being against you. This emotional chaos can sometimes lead to two extremes: feeling overwhelmed by your feelings or feeling totally numb to them.

Imagine you're at a concert. Your favorite band just hits the stage, and everyone around you is jumping and screaming with excitement. But you just stand there, feeling kind of "meh." That's emotional numbness. On the other hand, maybe you get into a fight with your best friend, and suddenly, you feel like you're gonna explode with anger and sadness. This is emotional overwhelm.

Both emotional overwhelm and numbness can be signs of trauma, which is a fancy way of saying you've been through something tough. Statistics show that nearly 70% of teens report experiencing at least one traumatic event in their lifetime! That's a lot of pressure to deal with. The good news is that there are skills you can learn to regulate your emotions and avoid getting stuck in either extreme.

SUPPRESED EMOTIONS MAY SHOW UP AS:

MILY GOMEZ, LPC @LATIBULECOUNSELING

Migranes	Skin rashes	Chronic pain	Hormonal imbalances
Tiredness	Digestive problems	Body tension	Diabetes
Constipation 	Heart disease	Trouble focusing 	Diarrhea
High blood pressure	Insomnia	Autoimmune disease	Memory problems

Sign & Symptoms of Emotional Numbness

Disconnecting from Loved Ones

Discomfort with Other's Emotions

Unaffected by Emotional Events

Pessimism About the Future

Inability to Laugh or Cry

Disinterest in Romance

Struggles with Expression

Disinterest in Hobbies

Feeling Flat or Empty Inside

EMOTIONAL NUMBNESS: FEELING FLAT?

Emotional numbness isn't just feeling "meh." It's a common sign of trauma or other mental health issues. While depression can cause numbness, it's not the only culprit.

Here's the key difference:

Depression is a condition, while numbness is a symptom.

Feeling disconnected? Unable to cry or even laugh? Imagine you and your BFF are having a huge fight. Normally, you'd be fuming or super sad, but instead, you feel strangely empty. Like the fight is happening on mute.

If this sounds familiar, then DON'T IGNORE IT!! Emotional numbness could be dimming your feelings.

Healthy Ways to Cope with Emotional Numbness

If numbness has you feeling disconnected, the following coping skills can help you tap back into life's flows:

Link Up with Your Peeps

Socializing with friends who've got your back is fuel. Meeting up, even for a small chat, can lift your spirits out of neutral.

Get Your Blood Pumping

Exercises like hoops or hiking release feel-good chemicals and energy to beat the flat feel. A jog around the block works wonders as well.

Find Your Flow

Yoga, art, gaming - activities that immerse your mind can help unlock what's beneath the surface level. Bonus points for creative outlets.

Catch Zen Rays

While mindfulness may sound basic, breathing deeply and living in the moment will activate subtler internal signals that numbness can dull.

Power Down for ZZZZ's

Quality shut eye ups the happy hormones while powering down stresses. Dark mode by 10, dudes!

Eat The Rainbow

Fuel your body with nutrients from fruits, veggies, and healthy fats. A wise diet improves both feelings and focus.

Reach Out for More Help

If coping kits aren't enough, ask guardians or school counselors how you can boost your tool belt. You've got this!

Write It Out

Journaling is a no-pressure way to process heavy feelings on paper. Keep pens moving to untangle messy emotions.

Pamper Yourself

Give self-care some love by taking a warm bath, trying a face mask, or listening to music — find soothing rituals to relax your mind and body.

Laugh It Off (With Friends)

Watching comedy videos together online or cracking jokes in person can release feel-good endorphins and lighten heavy moments.

Connect With Nature

Spending time outside amongst plants and critters is proven to lift moods. Bring a sketchpad to a park for a mindfulness boost.

Change Your Scenery

If usual spots spark blah vibes, check out a new café, bookstore, or trail for mental resuscitation. Field trips will flex your enthusiasm muscle.

Be Grateful (Seriously)

When numbness strikes, thankfulness training rewires grey matter. Keep a notes app to jot down things you appreciate, both big and small.

Know It's Not Permanent

Reaching out for help is brave. With coping skills and possibly time, your feelings highway will rev back up brighter than ever. This, too, shall pass.

Validation for Managing PTSD

Ever feel like you're stuck in a flashback loop? Maybe you had a crappy experience, and now certain things just trigger you out of nowhere. It's like your brain hits replay on the worst moments, and you're left feeling totally freaked out. This is a common reaction to trauma, which is a fancy way of saying you've been through something scary or upsetting.

Statistics show that teens are more likely to experience trauma than adults. That's a lot to deal with! The good news is that there

DRAW YOUR OWN PAIN SCALE

Feel like you hear too many comparisons of trauma?

Make a 0-10 scale sketching feelings and memories. Place your events on it without labels. Now do the same anonymously with friends. Chances are you'll realize none of us truly know another's personal pain threshold. We all have struggles, so spread compassion.

are ways to make sense of what happened and move forward in a healthy way. One powerful tool is none other than DBT. Think of it as a toolbox filled with skills to help you understand your emotions, manage stress, and build healthy relationships.

DBT teaches us that feelings are not always based on facts. With its emotion coaching tools, you can work through tough memories without letting them define you or scare you 24/7. Checking the facts is perfect for getting perspective when anxiety tries gaslighting your reality.

Plus, DBT groups feel like a safe zone to express yourself and realize you're not alone in how trauma has tweaked your brain. I used to think PTSD meant I was damaged, but now I see it simply as proof that I survived something huge.

You got this, friends. Reconciling hard memories is possible with patience and these evidence-based practices. Your reality is real, as is healing, so let's get you in tune with your feelings again!

Facing Trauma Head-On with Validation

When trauma messes with your brain, trusting your truth matters most. Here are some ways DBT can help you validate what's real for you:

Check Your Facts

Take a step back when anxiety gaslights your memories. Examine evidence to balance your perspective.

No Trauma Olympics

Don't compare cuts - all suffering deserves compassion. Your experiences shaped who you are in valid ways.

Share on Your Terms

Discussing trauma can be freeing with trustworthy souls. Be choosy and mindful of others' feelings, too, though, okay?

Build Your Safety Zone

If family or friends judge too harshly, set compassionate boundary lines together through calm explaining.

Love Your Inner Kid

That letter to the younger you is a reminder of how far you've come. Celebrate their strength and yours!

Keep on Learning

Triggers may stick around but handling them gets easier with practice. Growth happens even through hard times.

You've got this! With the right tools and your own wise guidance, reconcile tough memories in a caring way that empowers healing and living fully in present times. Stay true to yourself.

WRITE TO YOUR YOUNGER SELF

Need an uplifting pick-me-up?

Spend 5 minutes writing a letter to your past self at a time of struggles. Express pride in their strength overcoming difficult times. Let them know it's okay to have felt certain emotions. Promise brighter days ahead and that you'll always be there for support in the future. Revisiting this letter of comfort reminds you how far you've come in healing from trauma.

Self-Acceptance

Does it feel like you are your own worst critic? Deep down, you just can't catch a break from harsh thoughts about yourself. I'm here to tell you that there's a better way – by using mindfulness and radical acceptance.

Did you know that, on average, we think about 30,000 thoughts per day? And studies show that over 80% of teens' thoughts are negative self-talk. That's a lot of beating up on ourselves! The truth is that none of us are perfect. We all make mistakes and have things we'd like to change about who we are.

The cool thing about radical acceptance is that it teaches us that we don't have to agree with or like everything about ourselves to find peace. It's about noticing thoughts for what they are – just thoughts, not facts. And it's about accepting all our experiences, both good and bad, as what has shaped us into who we are today.

When we stop struggling so hard against ourselves and our past, we have more energy to be kind and take good care of those living inside these bodies and minds – ourselves! Trauma may always be part of our story, but it doesn't have to define us or our self-worth. We get to choose how much power we give it.

Want to try radical acceptance? Mindfulness exercises like breathing deeply or noticing nature with your senses can help reframe heavy thoughts. Be on the lookout for positive self-talk—we all deserve kindness from our own minds. You've got this!

Take Back Control of Your Inner Dialogue with DBT

Is your inner dialogue out of control? Like you're stuck on repeat crashing on yourself? We all have one - an internal voice that's constantly chattin' away in our heads. But for some, that mental monologue becomes an unwanted companion that just won't quit dumping on them. DBT can totally help shift that jam. Here, try these amazing methods:

Mindfulness & Acceptance 101

First, being aware of your thoughts is essential. Notice without judging what's playing in your head through meditation or grounding exercises.

Radical Rad Stuff

Then, work on seeing thoughts as just thoughts - not facts. Trauma may be part of your story, but it doesn't define you. Stress less about stuff you can't change.

Self-Esteem Effect

Did you know negative self-talk can wreck your vibe big time? On the other hand, treating yourself with compassion boosts how you feel overall.

Your Inner Critic

We all mess up sometimes, but harsh internal insults, aren't we? Clock how often that lil demon lies, and then chill it with positive self-affirmations.

Self-Care On Lock

DBT builds skills for relaxation and managing stress, so you feel good from the inside out. Treat yourself right, fam!

Relationships Re-up

Better handling relationships through clearer communication builds confidence in who you are and what you need. You got this!

It all starts with awareness, gang. With practice, DBT normalizes emotional crud and puts you in the driver's seat of your mental health road trip. Buckle up and enjoy the scenery - you're taking care of an awesome you!

---

5 MINUTE BREATHING BREAK

Stressed feeling like your thoughts are outta control?
Try this short exercise:
- Sit comfortably undisturbed
- Set timer for 5 minutes
- Inhale through nose, filling belly
- Exhale through pursed lips, empty lungs
- Focus only on breath's physical sensations
- Thoughts will come, gently return to breath
- As time ends, take final deep breath
- Notice any relaxation in body and calmer mind

This brief mindfulness meditation can help quiet a busy mind. Give it a try when you need a mental palate cleanser!

I hope this chapter has given you a good overview of how DBT can help you take back control of your inner dialogue and improve self-acceptance.

Remember, changing patterns of thought takes time and practice. Be patient with yourself as you work to incorporate DBT skills like mindfulness, radical acceptance, coping ahead, and relying on your wise mind rather than just your emotional mind.

This process of changing how you talk to yourself is empowering because it allows you to feel less at the mercy of your emotions. You have the power to soothe yourself and make choices that serve your well-being.

If you ever feel stuck or overwhelmed, remember that asking for help from people you trust is a sign of strength, not weakness. In the next chapter, we will discuss why learning DBT matters so much for handling life's challenges with more confidence and compassion for yourself and others. I'm rooting for you!

Key Takeaways

- Understand that many teens face traumatic experiences, and it's common to feel lost or overwhelmed after such events.
- Learn about DBT and how it can help teens cope with trauma by managing emotions, practicing distress tolerance, and using mindfulness techniques.
- Recognize that growth can occur after trauma, leading to increased resilience, new perspectives, and deeper connections with others.
- Outline steps such as naming the pain, learning from lessons, defining core values, using experiences to help others, and letting go of what can't be controlled.
- Understand the stages of change, from pre-contemplation to relapse, and utilize strategies to facilitate positive behavioral changes.

- Learn healthy coping skills for emotional numbness, such as socializing, exercise, mindfulness, and self-care practices.
- Validate traumatic experiences, check facts, avoid comparisons, share experiences on your terms, and build a supportive environment.
- Embrace radical acceptance and mindfulness to shift negative self-talk, acknowledge past experiences, and focus on self-care and positive affirmations.
- Utilize DBT techniques, such as mindfulness, radical acceptance, self-esteem building, and improving relationships, to manage inner dialogue and boost mental well-being.

CHAPTER 7

Unleashing Your Potential

"Wherever you go, there you are."

– Jon Kabat-Zinn

ET'S SAY YOU'RE scrolling through social media, and everyone seems to have it all together —perfect lives, perfect relationships, perfect grades.

But let's be real, that's not always how life feels, especially as a teenager. Emotions run high, things get messy, and sometimes you just wanna crawl under the covers and hide. But what if there was a way to navigate this emotional rollercoaster and live a life that feels good?

Well, DBT is all about teaching you tools and techniques for dealing with messy emotions. Think of it as a backpack filled with awesome tools to help you understand your feelings, manage stress, and build healthy relationships.

These skills teach you to build a strong relationship with yourself – seeing tough emotions as normal human stuff versus freak-outs, accepting mistakes gently, and soothing your inner good and bad chap. This balanced view frees up your mental energy to properly act when it counts.

Better yet, DBT groups help you realize you're not alone in how big life's stresses can seem. The more we support each other in practicing skills, the more confident we grow that no challenge is too huge to handle with time.

This chapter is about how learning to "check the facts" about thoughts and feelings — not just believing them blindly — gives you power over your path. It's time to toss out limiting beliefs like "there's no point; it's doomed to fail" and own your ability to plan strategically step-by-step.

The quote "Wherever you go, there you are" by Jon Kabat-Zinn means that no matter what situation you're in, you're always stuck with yourself. So why not learn how to get along with yourself better? That's what DBT can help you with!

DBT Improves Self-Efficacy

Ever feel like a passenger in your own life? With DBT, that changes. We learn to check facts versus feelings, soothing ourselves instead of drowning, and that we're not alone in our struggles.

Pretty soon, mistakes feel like learning, not failure. Deep breaths make stress way more manageable with problem-solving. Believing in yourself day by day gives freedom.

DBT's about to reveal your control - and set your confidence on fire! Four ways it boosts self-esteem:

Be Real with Yourself

Don't blame others or put yourself down. Give yourself positive self-talk instead. It's cool to make errors - that's how we grow. You're doing your best.

Say No Without Guilt

You don't need to apologize all the time. It's okay to set boundaries on your time and energy. Stick up for yourself without putting yourself down.

Follow What You Value

Figure out what really matters to you, like friends or school. Choose actions that fit your vision of you versus what others expect.

Speak Your Truth

Being real is freeing and brings you closer to people. White lies just stress you out. Decide your own story - make it true to you.

DBT takes effort but slowly reveals your power within. Keep practicing to feel better about being you!

THE TOP 10 ME CHALLENGE

To boost your self-esteem in under 5 minutes

Try This Now:

Ever wish you could flip a switch and suddenly feel awesome about yourself? Well now you totally can with this quick pick-me-up activity. Simply set a timer for 5 minutes and make a bulleted list of your top 10 qualities, skills, or things you dig about you. And here's the good part - next to each, share a brief example or story from your life that shows it off!

Once the buzzer goes off, give your list a read-through when you need an esteem boost. Need some inspo? How about your loyalty as a friend, awesome sense of humor, creativity, or kindness toward animals? The possibilities are endless, so take 5 and uncover your mega-talents! Not only will this have you celebrating your amazing qualities, but it's also a fun way to reframe any self-doubt. Try it - I promise you'll finish feeling like a superstar!

DBT in Social and Emotional Learning

School can feel like a jungle with classes, homework, and drama, right? It's easy to get overwhelmed and lash out. But what if there were healthy ways to handle frustrations and increase your chances of doing well? Enter DBT!

Managing emotions is key for smooth sailing in school and life. Let me give you the lowdown on proven strategies:

Social-Emotional Learning Classes

SEL focuses on social skills, feelings, communication, solving conflicts, and making good choices. Classes use fun activities to apply them daily. Studies show that SEL reduces stress and improves grades.

Therapy Groups

CBT and DBT group meetings typically last 6 to 12 weeks with counselors. Together, you'll recognize and challenge bad thought patterns, fueling emotions like "I'm dumb." Visuals help spot thoughts, feelings, and behavior in any moment.

One-on-One Counseling

Private talks with your counselor give space to share openly. You'll solve problems together and use relaxation techniques. Counselors are always there for you.

Emotion Apps

Apps like Calm, What's Up? And MindShift offer quick relaxation activities anywhere. This includes breathing, journaling, and playing games to teach new thinking. Free and only takes minutes daily.

The key is mixing lessons, groups, and coping tools for emotions and long-term success. You've got this!

THE EMOTIONS CHARADES GAME

Want to boost your self-control and social skills?
Try this quick activity:

- Set a timer for 5 minutes and have one person act out different emotions like happy, sad, angry, stressed without speaking. Can their partner correctly guess the feeling? Then switch roles.
  This silly charades game is a fun way to practice recognizing emotions - an important self-awareness skill many SEL programs focus on. Seeing how peers display certain feels helps you better spot them in yourself too!

- Once the buzzer goes, discuss - was it harder or easier than you thought? Which emotions were clearest? Try again with more specific emotions or scenarios next time.

This short game is a lighthearted way to build skills that can serve you well in relationships and schoolwork. Give it a try with friends - you might be surprised how much you can learn!

Learning DBT Skills Enhances Emotional Problem-Solving Teenagers

Ever feel like you're stuck in a cycle of negative thoughts and bad choices? Do you keep saying, "Ugh, I messed up again!" but nothing changes? Yeah, that's the same for most of us. The good news is that there are ways to break free from that pattern and feel better.

DBT is your secret weapon! Made for adults but tailored for teens now, too.

DBT helps us understand feelings better, so we don't feel overwhelmed. It gives strategies for coping when stressed without emotions spiraling. DBT also maintains good relationships by getting points across respectfully. Plus, self-awareness is needed to know what triggers us and other viewpoints.

Research shows that DBT is super effective! It empowers problem-solving instead of just reaction. DBT tools change behaviors and thoughts that may lead to acting out or feeling down. Who doesn't want more control, right?

If intense emotions or strained relationships are an issue, DBT can be the move. Ask your counselor about checking out a group - you may be surprised what these skills do for well-being and success. Ready to take back control? Time to level up with DBT!

DBT uses a bunch of cool techniques to help you with this. Here are a few of the best ones:

Mindfulness Techniques

Ever feel like you're on autopilot, just reacting to everything without even thinking? Mindfulness helps you take a step back and observe your emotions without judgment. Imagine your emotions as clouds passing by in the sky – you see them, but you don't get rained on!

> ***Scenario:*** Sarah's super mad because her friend canceled plans. DBT teaches her to take a moment, recognize her anger as a tightness in her chest, and label it as "anger" instead of exploding.

Emotional Regulation Techniques

Feeling overwhelmed by mood swings? DBT can help! You'll learn to track your emotions, identify what triggers them, and develop strategies to manage them in a healthy way.

> ***Scenario:*** Emma experiences frequent mood swings. Her therapist gives her a cheat sheet to track her emotions, figure out what sets her off, and find healthy ways to deal with them.

Distress Tolerance Techniques

Life throws curveballs, and sometimes, you just gotta deal with uncomfortable emotions. DBT teaches you ways to ride those waves instead of getting wiped out.

> ***Scenario:*** Alex struggles with self-harm urges. DBT teaches him to create a "comfort box" filled with his favorite things, like a soft blanket or a funny journal. When he feels overwhelmed, he uses these items to calm down instead of hurting himself.

Group Therapy

DBT group sessions are like a practice squad for real-life situations. You get to role-play scenarios with other teens and get feedback from your therapist.

Family Involvement

DBT isn't just for you! Your family can learn DBT skills, too, so they can support you at home. Think of it as a family training session for navigating teenage life together!

Creative Activities

Art therapy, music therapy, or journaling – DBT uses all sorts of fun activities to help you express yourself.

Digital Resources

There are even mindfulness apps and online platforms to help you practice your DBT skills on the go!

With DBT, you'll gain a toolbox filled with awesome skills to manage your emotions, make healthy choices, and build strong relationships. So, are you ready to level up your life skills and become the master of your teenage years? DBT can help!

DBT and Teenagers' Self-reported Social Resilience

Let's face it: Social life as a teen can feel like living in drama city. Between friendships, crushes, and family dynamics, things can get messy fast. You might feel overwhelmed by arguments with friends, stressed about fitting in, or anxious about talking to your crush. But hey, guess what? You're not alone! Everyone deals with social challenges, and the good news is there are tools to help you navigate them like a total pro.

This is where DBT comes in. It's a fancy way of saying a set of skills that can help you deal with tough emotions and situations, and guess what? Those skills translate perfectly to the social jungle.

Think of DBT skills as your personal superhero toolkit for building social resilience. They'll help you bounce back from tough situations, stay calm under pressure, and build stronger, healthier relationships with the people who matter most.

Level Up Your Social Resilience with DBT Skills

DBT provides a powerful toolset for handling drama like a pro. Some key techniques:

Mindfulness Techniques

Laser Focus: Learn to focus fully on friends without distractions. Builds stronger connections.

Emotion Regulation Strategies

Triggers and Healthier Responses: Spot what pushes your buttons and find better ways to react instead of just going with the mood.

Distress Tolerance Methods

Self-Soothing: Calm yourself with music or journaling instead of just reacting wildly during parties. Smoother social interactions ahead!

Interpersonal Effectiveness Tools

DEAR MAN: Use "I feel" statements to share how you feel without blaming. Research shows it decreases conflicts and increases understanding with your crew.

With regular practice of DBT skills, teenagers report a huge boost in social confidence and resilience. When tough times do happen, they feel secure facing issues instead of anxiously avoiding them.

Don't just take my word for it — try incorporating mindfulness, emotion regulation, distress tolerance, and interpersonal effectiveness techniques into your friend interactions. See how smoothly you can roll with typical teen twists and turns after leveling up your social skills with DBT!

With regular practice of these powerful DBT skills, you'll feel totally equipped to roll with whatever high school drama comes your way. Imagine the confidence you'll command in any social situation! Level up your resilience game and give these tips a try.

DBT truly offers a powerful toolkit for managing emotions and navigating social waters. While regular practice is required, research has shown that these skills boost self-efficacy and resilience over time.

BUFF YOUR SOCIAL SKILLS

Put mindfulness, emotion regulation, and conflict resolution to the test!

- Split into pairs and share an upcoming event you're feeling anxious about (ask, don't demand!). Listen fully with rapt attention focusing on words, not thoughts.
- Then reflect together using emotion regulation. Share what triggers your anxiety without blame. Brainstorm healthier responses you'll try instead.
- Change pairs and roleplay a disagreement over weekend plans using DEAR MAN. Say "I feel" calmly without raising your voice to find a solution.
- Take turns self-soothing during roleplay by squeezing stress balls or deep breathing to stay composed.

Test out these DBT moves in a judgment-free zone! See how they'll transform real-world interactions. Master these skills and you'll command any social situation like a pro. Are you ready to level up?

As you incorporate mindfulness, distress tolerance, emotion regulation, and interpersonal effectiveness techniques into your daily interactions, you'll find yourself a much calmer and more compassionate presence. Conflicts will faze you less while connections strengthen. Most importantly, you'll believe deeply in your ability to face life's challenges head-on.

Remember, every person deals with stress in their own way. DBT simply provides guidance to help you steer your ship smoothly. While the journey isn't quick, stay committed to this process of building mastery over self and relationships. You've so much greatness to offer the world.

With patience and heart, keep empowering your brilliant self. In the next chapter, we'll discuss how to continuously adapt and sustain DBT skills for lifelong well-being, growth, and success. Now go forth and be your wonderful!

Key Takeaways

- DBT equips teenagers with skills to understand and manage their emotions effectively, preventing them from feeling overwhelmed and out of control.
- DBT teaches strategies for building healthy relationships, including self-soothing techniques, conflict resolution skills, and effective communication methods like DEAR MAN.
- DBT helps teens develop a positive self-image by promoting fairness, encouraging assertiveness without guilt, aligning actions with personal values, and promoting honesty and authenticity.
- DBT offers practical tools like mindfulness techniques, emotional regulation strategies, distress tolerance methods, and interpersonal effectiveness tools to cope with stress, regulate emotions, and navigate social interactions smoothly.
- Integrating DBT skills into SEL classes, cognitive behavioral therapy groups, one-on-one counseling, and emotion-management apps enhances emotional problem-solving and supports long-term success in school and life.
- DBT empowers teenagers to take control of their lives, make positive changes in their thoughts and behaviors, and experience personal growth by learning and applying these valuable skills consistently.
- DBT skills boost social resilience by teaching mindfulness, emotion regulation, distress tolerance, and interpersonal effectiveness, leading to increased social confidence, smoother social interactions, and better conflict resolution skills.

CHAPTER 8

Sustaining Your Growth

"Do the best you can until you know better. Then, when you know better, do better."

– Maya Angelou

IMAGINE YOU JUST conquered a super tough video game level. You aced those boss battles and unlocked a whole new set of skills. Pretty awesome, right? But what if those skills just disappeared after you turned off the console? That wouldn't be cool!

Learning DBT skills is kind of like that. You've put in the effort to unlock these amazing tools for managing emotions, handling stress, and building healthy relationships. But just like with a video game, those skills won't stick around forever unless you keep practicing.

Studies show that around 80% of teens who participate in DBT programs experience significant improvements in their emotional well-being. That's a massive win! But the key word here is "practice." Those improvements only last if you keep using the DBT skills you learned in real-life situations.

The good news is that this chapter is your ultimate guide to mastering your DBT skills. Think of it as the ultimate cheat code for unlocking a happier, healthier you. I'll show you how to integrate these skills into your daily life so you can become a total DBT pro, ready to tackle any challenge that comes your way!

Optimizing Self-Care

Taking care of yourself is way more vital than you think. Shoutout to anyone who already knows self-care is the biz; you're totally right.

That mindfulness practice we do in DBT really helps you notice when neglecting yourself is bumming your mental wellness. It's like your brain's trying to tell you something needs TLC, and it's easy to miss the signs at first.

DBT teaches that our body, mind, and soul are all interconnected. Imagine trying to charge your phone while parts are detached – same deal with neglecting pieces of yourself! In most cases, stress causes physical issues first before feeling down sets in. So, making sure your mind stays fresh stops a ton of issues down the line.

A few years back, DBT taught me this big time. Learning about how my emotions and body interact was eye-opening. Suddenly, little things like relaxing more or eating better made a huge difference in my mental health. Wild, right?!

The best part of practicing mindfulness is how it programs your brain to automatically prioritize yourself now. Between stress relief tools and realizing that when you're running low, it's like you become your own wellness coach 24/7. So, carve out time each day to nourish yourself through simple self-care.

DBT Mindfulness: Your Secret Weapon for Chilling Out

Mindfulness is seriously key for regulating emotions. And after trying these easy strategies, I bet you will realize the power of mindsight. Here are four easy ways through which mindfulness can boost your emotional control:

1. Staying in the Moment

Worrying about tomorrow stresses you out, but with mindfulness, you can chill in the now. Less anxiety!

2. Strengthening Your Spotting Skills

Notice feelings ASAP so you can understand triggers rather than letting emotions surprise you. Then, use logic to stay grounded.

3. Maintaining Focus

Issues like anxiety affect attention, but mindfulness teaches concentration on the tasks or people that are important to you. More productivity ahead!

4. Being Hip to Your Environment

When stressed, everything feels weird, but mindfulness keeps you plugged into your surroundings. Rather than freaking out more, you can chill to solve what's up.

Basically, mindsight empowers you to own your emotions instead of letting them own you. Try meditating, deep breathing, or grounding exercises next time stress hits - I promise mindfulness will blow your mind. Level up that regulation game!

5. Establishing Routine

Building a daily routine can feel daunting, but trust me, it's worth the effort! As teenagers, we have a lot on our plates — school, extracurriculars, social lives, and the constant pressure to figure out what we want to do with our lives. It's no wonder that things can feel overwhelming at times. That's where DBT comes in to save the day.

FEELING STRESSED? TAKE A MINDFUL SHOWER!

Feeling overwhelmed? You don't need a spa day to find calm. Turn your next shower into a mini mindfulness retreat!

Try This:

- Set the Mood: Dim the lights, light a candle (if safe), and play calming music.
- Feel the Flow: Notice the temperature of the water as it hits your skin. Focus on the sensation as you lather up.
- Listen Deeply: Pay attention to the sounds of the water cascading, steam whooshing, and maybe even your own breathing.
- Breathe Deeply: Take slow, deliberate breaths in through your nose and out through your mouth. Feel your body relax with each exhale.
- Be Present: Let go of worries and to-do lists. Focus solely on the experience of showering, one mindful moment at a time.

This simple practice can help you de-stress, reconnect with yourself, and start your day (or end it!) feeling centered and calm. Give it a try and see how it washes your worries away!

Building a daily routine can feel daunting, but trust me, it's worth the effort! As teenagers, we have a lot on our plates—school, extracurriculars, social lives, and the constant pressure to figure out what we want to do with our lives. It's no wonder that things can feel overwhelming at times. That's where DBT comes in to save the day.

DBT is all about teaching us practical skills to manage our emotions, improve our relationships, and create a life worth living. And do you know what the secret ingredient is to really make those skills stick? Yep, you guessed it – a consistent routine! By setting up a daily schedule that incorporates DBT practices, we can turn these life-changing techniques into habits that become second nature.

Think about it this way – have you ever tried to learn a new skill, like playing an instrument or a sport, without practicing regularly? It's tough, right? The same goes for mastering the art of emotional regulation or interpersonal effectiveness. The more we incorporate these skills into our daily lives, the more natural and effortless they'll become.

So, where do we start? The key is to find a routine that works for you. Maybe that means setting aside 30 minutes every morning for mindfulness meditation or scheduling a weekly check-in with a trusted friend to practice your assertiveness skills. The beauty of DBT is that there's no one-size-fits-all approach – it's all about finding what clicks for you.

Remember, creating a healthy and sustainable routine takes time and experimentation. But trust me, the payoff is huge. So, let's get started on crafting a routine that will help you become the best version of yourself.

Routine Hacks to Sustain Mental Fitness for Life

Creating a good routine takes time to perfect. But DBT's got our backs with the ROUTINE system:

1. Responsibilities

First, list all your important responsibilities, such as school, family duties, and work—make sure to schedule these.

2. Ongoing Structure

Put everything on the calendar or set reminders so tasks aren't a blur. Crossing things off is satisfying AF.

3. Utilize DBT Skills

Carve out practice time for techniques. Being skilled up helps so much in tough moments.

4. Traditions

The crucial fun stuff! Game nights, movie dates, holidays - keep your faves on lock.

5. Interests Included

Make room for hobbies and curiosities, too. Want pottery? Research? Schedule them!

6. Novelty

Leave some breathing room, or your days get too strict. Chilling is essential sometimes.

ENVISION YOUR DREAM DAY

Curiosity is the catalyst for change, so boost yours.
- Take 10 minutes to scribble or journal your perfect day from waking to winding down.
- Include tangible activities and feelings you'd experience. Leave space for spontaneity too though.
- Now analyze - are your real routines getting you to this ideal?
- See mismatches clearly to tweak schedules toward your vision. Tiny habit shifts lead to whole transformations over time.

You deserve days that fulfill and energize you. One day is closer than you think when guided by clear vision and small consistent steps. Your best life awaits - will you start walking toward it today?

---

7. Envision a Satisfying life

Reassess your goals - is your routine helping you achieve your best future? Tweak it accordingly.

It takes trial and error to lock in your flow. But with ROUTINE as your guiding system, you got this in the bag!

Create a Support System

As a teen, life's wild ride can feel solo. But what if I said you don't have to go it alone? That's where a solid crew comes in.

Picture mentors who've lived it, allies who get you and a whole squad cheering you on. Sounds too good? Well, it's totally possible. Studies show that strong support improves your goals, coping skills, and confidence.

So, how do you build this legendary team? Put yourself out there - reach out to teachers you admire, join clubs to meet like minds, or chat with family/friends. Surround yourself with folks who understand without judging, offer advice when needed, and hype you up when tough. Pure magic, right?

A good squad helps big moves like speeches feel easier with cheerleaders. But support also navigates daily ups and downs. Need a vent sesh after a rough day? Your mentors got you. Struggling with homework? Your study buddy's there. Feeling lonely? Your ally's a text away.

So, what are you waiting for? Build your crew and unlock your full potential. Maybe you'll discover hidden talents along the way when motivated. Possibilities are endless with the right people by your side!

I've got step-by-step tips for finding peeps who push you to be your best. Keep reading and never feel alone again.

1. Identify Your Needs

Figure out if you need a shoulder, help, or motivation, and then find people who can fill those gaps.

2. Connect with Like-Minded Folks

Bond with others who share your interests through hobbies, teams, clubs, and online communities.

3. Seek Some Mentorship

Look for more experienced folks to learn from in areas you want to grow. Their skills and wisdom will help you elevate yourself.

4. Cultivate Relationships

Nurture relationships with family, friends, and other important peeps - these ties are key in the long run.

5. Be Vulnerable

Open up to trustworthy people about your feelings, thoughts, and challenges. Deeper connections mean better support all around.

6. Offer Support Too

Reliably lift up others - positive crews energize and assist each other in the long term.

Build your ideal support team and succeed way more with an awesome squad cheering you on!

SUPPORT SYSTEM CHECK-IN

Feeling like you could use some extra support lately?
- Take out your phone and set a reminder for weekly check-ins with your crew.
- Each time it goes off, shoot a text to one person from your squad. Ask how they're doing, share what's on your mind, and show your appreciation for their friendship.
- Not only will this strengthen your bonds, but research also shows that expressing gratitude boosts mood.
- Once a month, meet up with a member for coffee or an outing. Nourishing these relationships is key!

By intentionally devoting time to your support system, you'll feel much less alone facing whatever comes your way. Small investments reap big rewards - start building your village today.

Develop Realistic Goals and Monitor Progress

Hey friends, remember a few chapters back when we unpacked goal-setting strategies like making objectives measurable, starting small, and scheduling them for success? I won't recap all that wisdom here since you've already got it locked down - just wanted to remind you so you stay sharp with those insider hacks!

DEVELOPING YOUR LIFE WORTH LIVING GOALS
- *Reflect and discover:* Think on what really lights you up inside, like passions and values.
- *Set goals with purpose:* Now you know you - decide what changes you wanna see!
- *Make goals SMART:* Specific, Measurable, Attainable, Relevant and Time-based for success.

So let me tell you, having goals you feel capable of has seriously changed the game for me. No longer am I drowning in lofty Pinterest-worthy dreams that let me procrastinate forever. Now I'm accomplishing real things one small win at a time, and it's the best feeling ever!

Did you know achieving reachable goals reduces stress by over 25%? It goes to show setting yourself up for success is better for your well-being. I'm not freaking out as much now because obstacles don't feel like total roadblocks anymore.

Plus, the confidence boost you get from crossing things off your list?! It can be addictive to finish what you set out to do. Now, I'm not afraid to take on bigger projects because I know my methods work.

So, if you were sleeping on the goal-setting game, I hope your curiosity is piqued now! These smart, bite-sized habits will seriously change your life. No more excuses - you've got the tools, so do yourself a favor and level up already!

INTEGRATING AND SUSTAINING YOUR GOALS

- *Reference regularly:* Review your master plan and keep it fresh.
- *Evaluate and adapt:* Check your progress on the reg and tweak strategies as needed.
- *Continuous growth:* Your journey and dreams will evolve - embrace changing over time.

---

9 Awesome Perks of Killing It With Achievable Goals

By now, you should be in the groove of setting smart, meaningful goals. Creating goals that are worth living for takes some major self-reflection. Wanna know some dope benefits that come with having clearly mapped-out plans and tracking your progress? Stick around while I dish the deets!

1. Goals Give Direction & Focus

Having a purpose keeps you laser-targeted on leveling up without stressing over insignificant stuff.

2. Feeling that Sweet Accomplishment

Crossing things off your list makes your soul sing - dopamine on tap from chasing those wins!

3. Staying Motivated, Even When Life's Hard

Setbacks seem way smaller when you know you'll overcome them. Visualizing success keeps you in the game.

EXAMPLES OF LIFE WORTH LIVING GOALS

- Meaningful relationships: Bond with fam and friends.
- Personal growth: Continuously learn and explore through new hobbies or skills.
- Physical well-being: Prioritize workouts, nutrition, rest - treat your temple right.
- Career and success: Plan your dreams and steps to get there!
- Giving back: Find fulfilling causes and charities to contribute your gifts to.
- Emotional wellness: Activities that soothe your soul through chill times.
- Financial security: Savings-savvy strategies for independence.

4. Prioritizing Yourself

Figuring out what really fuels your fire helps max out your time on the right things.

5. A Realistic Plan for Dominating

Smartly schedule goals to make progress smooth and not feel overwhelmed.

6. Understanding Expectations Better

When your goals reflect YOUR vision, nothing's vague about where you're headed!

7. Preventing Overload

Breaking dreams into smaller pieces makes conquering them way less intimidating.

8. Clean Decision Making

Goals guide you toward choices that help your journey instead of leaving you perplexed.

9. Purpose That's Priceless

Tapping into your why on a deeper level gives you motivation for life!

So, what are you waiting for? Get after those goals already - your greatness awaits!

Applying the concepts in this chapter, such as establishing routines, cultivating support systems, and striving for achievable goals, is so important for sustaining mental well-being and progress made from DBT. Don't forget to celebrate the wins along the way—it feels good to acknowledge how far you've come! I'm excited to see what your bright future holds. In the next chapter, we'll explore envisioning your best self and life path using a DBT lens.

BOOST YOUR SELF-CARE POWER!

- Take a moment right now to do a quick self-care check-in. Close your eyes, take a deep breath, and **ask yourself**: *"What's one thing I can do today to nourish my mind, body, or soul?"*
- It could be as simple as taking a 5-minute walk outside, practicing a mindfulness meditation, or indulging in a favorite hobby. Commit to doing this self-care activity today and notice how it positively impacts your mood and well-being.

Ready to level up your self-care game? Give it a try and experience the immediate benefits firsthand!

Key Takeaways

- Just like mastering a video game, DBT skills require ongoing practice to maintain and improve. Regularly using these skills in real-life situations is essential for long-term emotional well-being.
- Mindfulness practice helps recognize signs of neglecting self-care and promotes overall mental wellness. Prioritizing self-care activities daily leads to better stress management and emotional regulation.
- Creating a daily routine that includes DBT practices helps make these skills a habit. The ROUTINE system (Responsibilities, Ongoing Structure, Utilize DBT Skills, Traditions, Interests Included, Novelty, and Envision a Satisfying Life) can guide you in building a sustainable routine for mental fitness.
- Building a strong support system with mentors, like-minded individuals, and trusted allies helps in achieving goals, maintaining healthy coping strategies, and feeling empowered during challenges.

- Setting achievable goals, monitoring progress, and celebrating small wins reduces stress, boosts confidence, and keeps motivation high. Smart goal setting leads to focused direction, prioritization, and better decision-making.

CHAPTER 9

Envisage Your Future

> *"We can't become what we need to be by remaining what we are."*
>
> **– Oprah Winfrey**

ISN'T THAT THE truth, guys? As teenagers, you are at a pivotal point in your life – standing on the edge of the unknown with the future stretching out before you like a blank canvas. It can feel equal parts exciting and terrifying, am I right?

But what if I told you that you don't have to face that future alone? With the power of DBT in your toolkit, you can not only survive life's curveballs but thrive in the face of them. Yep, you heard me right – this chapter is your road map to becoming the best version of yourself, no matter what challenges come your way.

Think about it this way: When you have the essential skills to manage your emotions, build healthy relationships, and create a life worth living, suddenly, nothing seems too big to tackle — feeling anxious about that big presentation? Your mindfulness techniques have got your back. Struggling to communicate your needs to your parents? Your assertiveness skills will save the day. Hitting a rough patch and needing to refocus on self-care? Your crisis survival strategies are there to pick you up.

The bottom line is that by investing in your personal growth now, you're setting yourself up for a lifetime of success and fulfillment. Gone are the days of feeling lost, overwhelmed, or unprepared for the next chapter. With DBT as your trusty sidekick, you'll be able to not just survive but thrive in the face of whatever the future holds.

And who knows, you might even surprise yourself along the way. Maybe you'll discover a hidden talent or passion you never knew you had. Or perhaps you'll find the courage to take a leap and pursue a dream that used to feel totally out of reach. The possibilities are truly endless when you've got the right tools and the right mindset in your corner.

Fulfilling Your Potential

You've probably heard how the only constant is change, right? As teens, you're transforming like crazy inside and out. Interests, dreams, and even who you are will look different in just a few years.

Crazy to think how different life may be down the line! But that's also so cool - it means your potential is endless, and your story's still unfolding.

Right now, everything feels uncertain. You've got ideas for careers, places to visit, relationships...but I promise these will evolve with new passions and experiences. Half of grads even work outside their major! Just shows how unpredictable the future can get.

But change doesn't have to stress you - it means limitless potential and reinventing yourself wherever life leads.

TEST YOUR EMOTIONAL IQ

How hip are you to your feelings? Let's find out!

Set a timer for 3 minutes and jot down as many emotions as you can think of - good, bad, and everything in between.

Did you name a wide range? Struggle to think of any?

Now's your chance to boost your emotional vocabulary using DBT. The more labels you can assign to how you're feeling, the easier it'll be to regulate yourself like a pro.

Happy emotional detecting!

This is where DBT comes in clutch. It teaches flexibility and preparing for uncertainty. DBT gives strategies to imagine multiple futures while also accepting plans may vary. You'll see change not as a threat but as an adventure.

Embracing transformation with DBT means riding the waves of whatever's next with confidence. Your story's just getting started!

How DBT Can Make You a Superhero

Want to know some cool ways that learning DBT could totally transform your life for the better?

I will now share how focusing on your evolving aspirations through a DBT lens can help you welcome potential opportunities that come your way. So, keep reading to gain a whole new perspective on what's ahead - I have a feeling you'll be stoked!

Emotional Control 101

DBT teaches you to get in touch with your feelings and regulate them like a pro. You'll notice triggers quicker and handle them in healthier ways — no more emotional chaos!

Relationship Goals

The communication skills you will learn through DBT will help you build stronger bonds with friends and family. With tight communication skills and boundaries from DBT, saying what you mean gets easier, and drama fades — a win-win situation for chill relationships all around.

Stress, Who?

Distress tolerance teaches relaxation hacks to keep you Zen when life's nutty. No need to freak - you'll cope like a champ without risky moves.

Negative Thoughts, Begone!

By catching those unhelpful thoughts, DBT switches up your mindset for good vibes only. Positivity powers up everything.

Habits on Lock

Learning to manage stress stops harmful habits and keeps you ballin' on your goals long-run. You totally got this, dawg!

So yeah, these skills are practically magic. I hope trying DBT sounds even more intriguing now that you know it could literally transform your life into a happier one.

Understand and Own Emotions

Ever had feelings ruin your mood out of nowhere? It's like one minute you're doing great, then emotions take the wheel. That's no good! Understanding feelings is key to being in control.

Emotions impact everything from relationships to challenges. If you don't know what's really upsetting you, it's easy to act out or doubt yourself. Before you know it, small things derail your plans!

DBT teaches being fully present with emotions - like watching from far away without judgment. Studies show this

EMOTION CHECK-IN ACTIVITY:

Pause for a moment and tune in to your feelings.

- Take a deep breath and ask yourself: *What am I feeling right now?*

- Give a name to your emotion, whether it's joy, frustration, excitement, or something else.

This simple practice of acknowledging your feelings can enhance self-awareness and pave the way for better emotional regulation.

helps 87% feel less stressed. Once you pay attention, taking back control gets easier. You navigate emotions in healthier ways and become the boss!

It's time to level up that emotional intuition ASAP. Your potential is calling - and mastering feelings is the wave. Ready to uncover the truth about emotions? Keep reading!

Emotions Evolved

Emotions aren't random - they come from evolution! Scientists have found that basic emotions like anger, fear, and happiness help us make decisions and survive dangers like cliffs.

Emotions and Decision-Making

Believe it, feelings play a huge role in choices. They help assign value to info, steering us one way or another. Understanding this connection makes you great at deciding.

Emotional Disorders

Like any body part, emotions can get out of whack sometimes. Conditions like depression and anxiety cause intense or long feelings impacting daily life. But with support, you can manage emotions and thrive.

The Bottom Line

Feelings are a gift, not a curse. Study emotions to boost confidence in handling moods as challenges come up. Learn how feelings work - it levels up LIFE SKILLS big time!

Wanna Decode Your Feelings?

Ever wonder why you feel jittery before a big game or your stomach flips when you see your crush? Our emotions can be confusing sometimes, but hey, there's a way to crack the code!

This quick guide will help you understand your emotions better. Let's get started!

Recognize Anger

Anger is that hot, tense feeling you get when someone does something wrong to you. It might start in your back and travel up to your neck and jaw. You might feel flushed and on edge. Anger is your body's way of telling you that you need to stand up for yourself.

Spot Disgust

Ew, gross! Disgust is that queasy, nauseous feeling you get when you encounter something revolting, like rotten food or a moral violation. You might scrunch up your nose and want to back away from the yucky thing.

Feel the Fear

Fear is that racing heart, sweaty palms, and jittery feeling you get when you're faced with a real threat, like a scary dog or a bully. Your body is trying to get you to fight or flee to stay safe.

Recognize Happiness

Ah, the good stuff! Happiness can feel warm and tingly all over your body. You might feel content, safe, and like you're living your best life.

Identify Sadness

Sadness often starts in your chest, like a heaviness, and moves up to your throat and eyes, where the tears come. Allowing yourself to fully feel and express sadness can be cleansing after a loss.

Notice Surprise

Surprise is that little jolt you feel when something unexpected happens, but it's not a threat. It's your brain's way of re-focusing your attention on something new.

FEELING EXPLORER

Ever wonder where exactly emotions live inside you? Do some deep diving into four core feels with this hands-on activity.

1. *Anger* – Think of a time you were mad. Where do you notice tension rising?
2. *Disgust* – Picture something gross. Can you feel the ick in your stomach?
3. *Fear* – Recall a scary moment. Feel your heart racing yet?
4. *Happiness* – Remember a fun time. Smile as the warmth spreads!

Take 5 minutes to fully experience each emotion in your body. Jot down any patterns you noticed. With practice, you'll get fluent in the physical language of feelings. Now go get acquainted with your emotional landscape from the inside out!

Give this mind-body meditation a try to level up your awareness of what different feelings physically feel like. Reporting back what you discover trains your brain to better understand emotion.

Okay, now it's your turn! Try paying attention to how your body feels when you experience different emotions. See if you can identify the unique sensations for each one. This practice will help you become a pro at recognizing your feelings. Let me know how it goes!

Reduce Emotional Vulnerability

Ever feel like your heart's been straight-up shattered into a million pieces? Hey, break-ups are brutal, but you know what makes them even worse? Going into relationships, putting all your feelings on full display.

When you bare your soul only to get left in the dust, that's pure agony.

I'm not saying you gotta build some steel wall around your heart 24/7 - shows of emotion are important parts of living! But handing full control of your emotions to another person is setting yourself up to get majorly played. Trust me, I've been there and done that; I still have the shreds of a T-shirt to prove it, lol.

Now I know what you're thinking - how can you even have a real connection if you don't pour your heart out?

Totally valid. You DO want intimacy, vulnerability, and trust in a relationship. But slowly easing into emotional openness at a healthy pace is smart, not stupid. Save the soul-baring love confessions for when you really know someone has your back. Do you feel me?

Start by paying attention to how a person makes you feel. Do they seem interested in getting to know YOU, or are they trying to swoop in for the save? Move at the speed of trust. And know that keeping a little guard up till you're sure is the cooler play if you don't want to be left in bits and pieces all over the floor! Who's trying to be somebody's emotional scratching post anyway, am I right?

I know managing big feelings is no joke, and that's where DBT comes in - it gives us real tools to feel better.

POSITIVE PICKS TO PROCESS YOUR VIBES

- Chat with your squad
- Get your heart pumping at the gym
- Vent in a journal
- Zen out with meditation
- Therapy can help too
- Doctor yourself up when you're under the weather
- Catch Z's - sleep is bomb for your brain
- Notice negative thoughts making you mad
- Give yourself a time out when overwhelmed

FEELING FIXES THAT'LL ONLY BACKFIRE

- Boozing or doing drugs
- Hurting yourself on purpose
- Avoiding stuff that makes you mad
- Lashing out angry
- Constant social media when you should sleep

Here are a few things you should do for your emotional boost:

Name That Feeling

As I have said before, DBT teaches us to label our exact emotions, like "frustrated" instead of just "bad." Knowing what you feel is the first step to handling it better.

Get Present

Mindfulness means living in the now instead of past mistakes or future worries. Grounding techniques keep you anchored to the present moment.

Release The Pain

Even negative vibes need to be felt and flowed through instead of fighting them. Imagery, like waves rolling through, can help release what's bothering you.

Take Care Of You

To handle emotions straight, your body needs self-love through sleep, food, exercise, and chill time. Take good care of your temple!

Get Happy Too

It's easy to focus on sad feelings, but happiness is just as important. Make room for joy during celebrations through fun activities and quality time with people who resonate with you.

Those are some dope DBT tools to feel better and ride the emotion rollercoaster with more balance. Give them a try next time your feelings are on 100.

STOPP!!

When those big feelings start rocking, it's time for **STOPP.**
This quick technique will help you press pause on intense emotions so you can ride them out in a chill way. **Just remember the letters:**

- **S** - Stop! Put the brakes on that feeling before it runs you over.
- **T** - Take a breath. In and out to calm your body down.
- **O** - Observe what's up. Check your thoughts, focus, what/who you're reacting to, feels in your body.
- **P** - Pull back. Get some perspective on the big pic. What would your BFF say to reassure you?
- **P** - Proceed wisely. Now you see clearly - how can you handle this in a way that makes you feel validated still?

Try STOPPing the next time emotions get overwhelming. Those few seconds to reflect will make all the difference in keeping your cool.

Spread A Positive Mindset

I have a question for you all. Have you ever noticed how being pumped about something gets others pumped, too? Well, you know, spreading good vibes is good for our mental health. For real! Having a positive mindset doesn't just benefit those around you - it benefits YOU too.

CHILL VIBES ATTRACT CHILL PEOPLE:

When you're calm and collected, people are more likely to listen to what you have to say. Think about it, would you rather take advice from someone freaking out or someone who's got a handle on things? Exactly! Mindfulness helps you stay cool, so your friends will be more open to hearing about the benefits of DBT.

Research shows that mindfulness practices like gratitude journaling and focusing on the present moment can help reduce stress and depression in teens just like us. One easy way to sneak more mindfulness into your day is by telling others about cool concepts you've learned, like DBT.

WALKING THE WALK, NOT JUST TALKING THE TALK:

DBT is all about managing emotions in healthy ways. By practicing mindfulness yourself, you're showing your friends that DBT actually works! It's like living proof that you can take control of your feelings and not the other way around.

DBT skills are all about healthily managing tough emotions. When you explain some of the skills to friends - like what primary emotions are or labeling your feelings specifically - you also reflect on them. Practicing gratitude by thinking of three good things that happened each day is another mindfulness technique you can teach your squad.

So next time someone's stressed about a test or feeling down, share some hope by explaining how DBT could help refocus their thoughts. Who knows, you might end up using the skill to calm your own nerves, too!

Having a positive outlook is contagious - it fuels motivation and stronger connections. So spread that good energy whenever you get a chance. Your wellness and everyone else's are all connected.

Next time a homie needs a pick me up, give them some mindfulness inspiration. Remind them they've got this and that better feels are possible with a bit of self-care and presence. You never know - your words could change their mindset for good!

But before that, let's look at some excellent mindfulness techniques worth sharing with others.

Breathe And Be

Focusing on your breathing is always a good start. Sit up straight, close your eyes, and focus on your breath moving in and out. It's a simple but powerful way to reset your mind and body.

Walk It Out

Take a mindful nature walk and really notice all the cool sights, sounds, and smells around you. Feel each step on the ground. Next time you need a mental break, go for a mindful stroll. Notice the flutter of leaves, the feel of the ground, and the sounds around you—instant refresh.

Eat With Intention

Instead of just wolfing down your food, take the time to appreciate the flavors, textures, and where the ingredients came from. Cultivates gratitude. Slow down at mealtimes and enjoy every bite. Think about where the food came from. Notice colors and flavors fully.

Ground Yourself

Take a moment to notice what's happening with all five senses. When your mind is scattered, engage your five senses. What can you see, hear, smell, taste, and touch right now? This simple exercise brings you back to the present. It helps calm your mind.

Body Scan

Lay back, close your eyes, take some deep breaths, and systematically relax each part of your body. It's a full body reset button that melts away tension.

Hand Over Heart

Sit straight, close your eyes, and place your hand on your heart; feel it beating. Breathe deep and bring awareness to your breath. This quick practice can help dissolve stress anytime, anywhere.

Palm Reading (No Fortune-Telling Required)

Trace the lines in your hand slowly, noticing how it feels. It's a simple yet powerful way to ground yourself in the present moment.

Drive Calm

Instead of zoning out behind the wheel, be aware of your actions and the road. When chilling in the car, focus on your driving and let other cars slide. Letting go of distractions makes you a calmer, safer driver. You'll feel less stressed.

Try one of these simple mindfulness practices next time stress is getting you or any of your pals. They'll help you stay present and feel more at peace.

This chapter explored how DBT can help you envision your future and reach your fullest potential. By strengthening your emotional regulation, communication skills, and ability to manage stress, you gain powerful tools to face whatever challenges come your way confidently.

The future may feel uncertain, but with DBT in your toolbox, you have everything you need to not just survive but thrive.

In the upcoming last chapter, we will conclude the book by exploring how you can become the best version of yourself possible through applying the principles of DBT to your daily life. We'll look at staying true to who you are while also constantly growing into the next phase of your life. Achieving self-mastery is an ongoing process, but making DBT a habit now will serve you well for many years to come as your interests, values, and dreams continue to evolve.

BREATHE, NOTICE, RELEASE MINDFULNESS EXERCISE:

- Sit comfortably with your back straight but not stiff.
- Close your eyes and bring your attention to your breathing.
- Feel your belly rise on the inhale and fall on the exhale.
- Notice any physical sensations, emotions, or thoughts.
- Gently observe them without judgment.
- On the exhale, imagine releasing anything causing stress.
- Repeat for 5-10 minutes, focusing only on your breath.
- When your mind wanders, no problems - softly guide it back.
- Finish by noticing how your body feels, from your head to toes.
- See if you can carry this relaxed yet aware state with you.
- It's a simple way to reduce stress anytime, anywhere.

Give it a try and see if you feel any calmer afterwards! This quick practice can help clear your mind throughout your busy day.

Key Takeaways

- Utilize DBT skills to navigate life's challenges and thrive, turning uncertainty into opportunity.
- Understand that change is constant and embrace it as an adventure, allowing for endless possibilities and personal growth.
- Learn to identify, understand, and regulate your emotions effectively using DBT techniques, empowering yourself to stay in control.
- Develop strong communication skills, set healthy boundaries, and cultivate meaningful connections to support your well-being.
- Create achievable goals, track your progress, and celebrate small wins, reducing stress and boosting motivation.
- Incorporate mindfulness into your daily life through simple exercises, enhancing emotional resilience and overall well-being.

CHAPTER 10

Embracing Your Best Self

> *"Change equals self-improvement. Push yourself to places you haven't been before."*
>
> **– Pat Summitt**

YOU HAVE COME so far in this journey of learning about yourself and developing important life skills. As teens, every day brings new experiences that help shape who you're becoming. While change can be scary sometimes, it also presents exciting opportunities for growth.

Did you know that the teenage brain is still developing well into your twenties? That means you have so much potential to transform yourself during these formative years. I find that really empowering - you get to directly influence how your future turns out. With the right mindset and tools like DBT, the best is yet to come!

As we wrap up our time together, I want to leave you with this thought: In 10 years, you will have changed in many ways, for better or worse, based on the choices you make today. The beauty is that DBT gives you strategies to actively steer your life in a positive direction. You don't have to be a passenger in your own story - you have the power to write the next chapter however you want. Sounds cool, right?

I truly believe that if you commit to continual self-improvement, striving to be just a little bit better each day, there are no limits to how awesome your life can turn out. Are you ready to level up and become your best self yet? Keep reading to uncover a straightforward plan for shaping your brightest future.

Celebration Station

You know accomplishments feel better when you take a second to appreciate them, right? Whether an A on a big test or sticking to regular exercising, celebrating keeps spirits up.

Treating yourself after milestones, big or small, is important. Hitting pause to hype yourself up or tell friends reminds you how far you've come. It feels good to see hard work paying off!

I'm not saying to throw parties to do chores, haha. Even simple recognition, like writing in a gratitude journal or your fave dessert, is enough to boost confidence. The key is noting progress to see continued growth.

WHAT'S THE DEAL WITH SMALL WINS?

We've all heard that quote by Edison about failing 10,000 times - but did you know he wasn't really failing at all? Each of those "failures" was progress toward his goal of inventing the lightbulb. That's what small wins are all about.

A small win is any accomplishment, no matter how little, that moves you forward. Got a B on your history quiz instead of a C like usual? Small win! Stuck to your workout for a whole week straight? Heck yeah, celebrate that small win! They add up over time.

As teens, you've got a lot on your plates. Celebrating large and small wins reminds us we're crushing it on tough days. It gives mini motivation boosts to keep moving toward goals. Next time you level up, pat yourself on the back - you deserve it!

We all want to reach the top, but momentum is hard to keep. That's where celebrating wins comes HUGE. I'm sharing strategies to fuel your motivation to climb to success. So, here are some key ways to celebrate those small wins:

Break It Down

Setting massive goals can feel impossible. Break them into smaller, achievable steps instead. Focus on knocking those out one by one.

Treat Yourself

Decide how you're gonna celebrate reaching each mini milestone. Extra screen time for finishing that paper? Ice cream date after acing your exam? A little reward keeps the motivation flowing.

Track That Progress

Nothing feels better than seeing how far you've come. Keep a journal tracking your goals and check those accomplishments off. Snap a pic of the completed sections to look back on. Visual reminders of your hard work boost confidence.

Don't underestimate the tiny wins. Recruiting friends for your school's charity walk? Small win. Practicing your presentation without stuttering? Another win. Building healthy habits and achieving goals is a marathon, not a sprint. Enjoying little celebratory checkpoints along the way makes the overall journey way more fun. Stay focused on progress over perfection, and you'll be cruising in no time. You've got this!

DEVELOP POWERFUL HABITS

Celebrating small wins is key to forming habits that will seriously benefit you long-run. Scientists say it takes around 60 days to make something a regular part of your routine. But changing takes small steps each day. Read one chapter of that book instead of quitting after one paragraph? Reward yourself, look how far you've come already!

144

Review of Important DBT Skills:

Alright, guys, we've come a long way since starting this DBT journey. Remember way back when we first learned core skills like mindfulness, emotion regulation, and distress tolerance? It's crazy to think how much more equipped we are now to face life's challenges.

I know how overwhelmed and unsure you all must have felt about learning these new concepts. I hope that now you all have realized that all these hours of practicing mindfulness, emotional regulation, and effective communication will pay you off in the future.

NATURE MINDFULNESS:

Sit outside and observe:
5 things you see,
4 things you feel,
3 things you hear,
2 things you smell,
1 thing you taste.

BODY SCAN:

Sit comfortably and focus on each body part, one by one, noticing any sensations.

Well, now you know how using DBT skills can change your brain. Actions like mindful breathing and walking boost areas related to focus and self-control. Distress tolerance hacks like positive self-talk decrease reactivity in stressful moments. Practicing interpersonal effectiveness regularly strengthens communication circuits in the brain.

It is pretty cool how the dedicated use of these evidence-based skills physically improves our ability to thrive. No wonder DBT is so awesome - it quite literally builds our emotional intelligence over time. As we wrap things up, let's do a quick mental recap of mindfulness, emotion regulation, distress tolerance, and interpersonal effectiveness. Let's review what we've covered so far, shall we?

Mindfulness: The Art of Living in the Present

Mindfulness is all about being fully present and aware instead of getting caught up in the past or worrying about the future. It's like having a superpower that allows you to tune into the here and now. We talked about the "what" skills, like observing, describing, and participating, as well as the "how" skills, like being non-judgmental and one-mindful. The goal? Developing that sweet spot between emotion and reason, also known as your "wise mind."

TRY THIS MINDFUL MOMENT!!

The next time you're feeling stressed, take a break and try this simple mindfulness exercise. Find a quiet spot, close your eyes, and focus on your breathing. Notice the sensation of air moving in and out of your body. When your mind wanders, gently bring your attention back to your breath. Do this for just 2-3 minutes and feel the tension melt away.

Interpersonal Effectiveness: Leveling Up Your Relationships

Interpersonal effectiveness is about learning how to speak up for your needs, set boundaries, and respect yourself - all while keeping your relationships strong and healthy. Whether it's saying no, asking for what you want, or maintaining self-respect, these skills are gonna be your new best friends.

COMPLIMENT SWAP:

Take turns giving genuine compliments to build each other up.

ASSERTIVENESS ROLE-PLAY:

Act out scenarios where you need to stick up for yourself and get feedback.

PRACTICE ASSERTIVE COMMUNICATION

The next time you need to have a tough conversation, try using the DEAR MAN method.

D - Describe the situation,

E - Express your feelings,

A - Assert your needs,

R - Reinforce the positives,

M - Stay mindful, and

N - Negotiate.

This approach can help you communicate effectively without jeopardizing the relationship.

Distress Tolerance: Riding the Wave of Tough Emotions

Distress tolerance is like having a toolkit full of coping mechanisms for when life gets tough. We covered things like grounding techniques, radical acceptance, and just letting yourself feel those emotions without getting swept away. The idea is to ride out the storm rather than trying to control the uncontrollable.

CREATE A COPING SKILLS BOX

Assemble a box or jar filled with small items that can help soothe you when you're feeling overwhelmed. This could include stress balls, essential oils, inspirational notes, or anything else that brings you comfort. Whenever you need a quick pick-me-up, reach for your personalized coping skills box.

Emotional Regulation: Mastering Your Feelings

Finally, emotional regulation is all about taking charge of your own emotions, rather than letting them control you. You learned skills like reality-checking, acceptance, and even doing the opposite of what your emotions are telling you to do. No more emotional rollercoasters, my friends!

TRY THE STOPP TECHNIQUE

When you notice a strong emotion arising, use the STOPP technique. S - Stop what you're doing, T - Take a few deep breaths, O - Observe your thoughts and feelings without judgment, P - Pull back and think about the bigger picture, P - Proceed mindfully. This simple practice can interrupt the cycle of reactivity and help you respond more skillfully.

Remember, these DBT superpowers take practice, but the payoff is huge. You'll be handling life's challenges with consistency and dedication like a total pro. So, keep exploring, experimenting, and, most importantly, be kind to yourself along the way. Your future self is counting on you!

Cultivating and Embracing DBT

We've put in the work learning all these dope DBT skills. But the fun isn't over yet - now it's time to level up how you apply them for real. Did you know keeping skills sharp is one of the best ways to protect your mental health long term? According to one study, practicing emotion regulation strategies daily lowered depression and anxiety after just one month. Pretty sweet, right?

My tip is to treat your new emotional toolkit like your fave video game. You wouldn't just play through once and never pick it up again; you'd keep grinding to unlock new levels and achievements. Same thing here - the more you use your mindfulness, distress tolerance, and other abilities, the more they'll be second nature when life throws curveballs. Keep a skills journal, set weekly goals to try different techniques, or come up with codes for texting friends when you need a DBT buddy.

Remember, cultivating emotional intelligence is a lifelong quest, not something you "finish." I believe you guys can flex those new strengths. So, what are you waiting for? Go dominate your emotions like the champions you are!

Distress Tolerance 101: Your Toolkit for Intense Emotions

When big feelings start swirling, it's hard to stay calm and think straight. You just want to scream, cry, or smash stuff until the storm passes. But before you do something you'll regret; promise me you'll try taking a few deep breaths.

I know handling emotions is easier said than done but try these simple DBT distress tolerance techniques next time you're about to lose your cool. Just a few minutes of TIPP skills, IMPROVE strategies, or ACCEPTS activities can be all it takes to ride the wave instead of wiping it out. What have you got to lose, right?

So, next time you feel yourself starting to unravel, pause and put these practices to the test. I guarantee they'll give you a new perspective, even on the worst of days. Trust me - don't let your emotions call all the shots until you've given these bad boys a try.

Get Your Distract On

When you're feeling totally stressed or upset, one of the best things you can do is distract yourself. That could mean watching your favorite movie, playing a video game, or even calling up a friend to chat. The key is to find something that really grabs your attention and takes your mind off the tough stuff.

Soothe Yourself

Another awesome skill is "self-soothing." This is all about using your five senses to calm yourself down. Maybe that's taking a warm bath, listening to relaxing music, or surrounding yourself with a comfy, cozy environment. The goal is to give your mind and body a little TLC.

The IMPROVE Method

This one's a real Swiss Army knife of skills! IMPROVE stands for Imagery, Meaning, Prayer/Spirituality, Relaxation, One thing at a time, Vacation, and Encouragement. By using a mix of these techniques, you can totally shift your mindset and make a tough situation more bearable.

Weigh the Pros and Cons

Sometimes, when you're feeling super stressed, it can be hard to see the bigger picture. That's where the "Pros and Cons" skill comes in. It's all about taking a step back and carefully considering the potential upsides and downsides of different choices. This can help you make better decisions, even when your emotions are running high.

Get Physical with TIPP

TIPP is a set of physical strategies that can quickly calm you down. It stands for Temperature change (like holding an ice pack), Intense exercise, Paced breathing, and Progressive muscle relaxation. By using your body, you can reduce the intensity of those overwhelming emotions.

Converting Knowledge into Action

Let's be real for a second, my friends - knowing about awesome coping skills like the ones in DBT is great and all, but if you don't put them into practice, they're pretty much useless. It's kind of like having a secret superhero toolbox but never opening it up to use the cool gadgets inside.

See, the thing is, when life gets tough and intense emotions start to take over, these DBT skills can be absolute game-changers. But they only work if you make them a part of your regular routine. It's all about taking that knowledge and turning it into real-world action — that's where the magic happens!

Imagine riding the emotional rollercoaster with confidence, quickly soothing yourself when things get overwhelming, or navigating tough decisions with clarity. That's the power of using DBT skills. And the best part? It's not as complicated as it might sound. In fact, with a little bit of practice and an open mindset, you can start seeing the benefits almost immediately.

So, my awesome teen friends, are you ready to unlock your inner superhero? It's time to dive in, experiment, and discover which DBT skills resonate with you the most. Trust me, your future self will thank you for making the effort. After all, knowledge is power, but action is where the real transformation begins.

3 Problems Blocking Your Progress - And How to One-Hit K.O. Them

We all wanna better ourselves, right? But actually, doing it is another story. Here are the biggest hurdles to taking action and simple ways to vault over them

Problem #1 - Thinking Big Changes = Big Gains

We think we gotta remake ourselves completely to grow. But going huge causes overwhelm fast. Starting small makes success way more likely.

Solution - Make Tiny Adjustments

Focus on mini improvements you can absolutely nail. Meditate for 5 mins instead of 30. Hit the gym twice a week, not daily. Little wins add up over time, no sweat!

Problem #2 - Winging It Without a Plan

Vague goals like "get healthy" don't do anything. But with a schedule, you're way more accountable.

Solution - Detail It Out

Map out the small actions you'll take each week. When will you hit the books? Which days are for working out? Planning rules.

Problem #3 - Forgetting Skills in the Moment

We soak up self-help info but blank when stressed. Notes and reminders save us.

Solution - Take Notes, Set Triggers

Jot down key lessons. Then, set cues like times, locations, or feelings to apply them as needed. Knowledge, meet action!

Break barriers between knowing and doing with these simple tweaks. You got this!

"ACCEPTS" CHALLENGE!

If nothing from above works for you, try this ultimate skill:

When you're struggling with intense emotions, the "ACCEPTS" skill can be a game-changer. It offers a variety of tools to help you manage distress, so give it a try and see what works best for you.

The **"ACCEPTS"** Challenge:

- **A** - Activities: Engage in a positive, absorbing activity to shift your focus.
- **C** - Contributing: Do something to help others and take the attention off yourself.
- **C** - Comparisons: Reflect on times you've overcome bigger challenges.
- **E** - Emotions: Intentionally do something that elicits the opposite emotion.
- **P** - Pushing Away: Visualize putting your distressing thoughts in a mental "box."
- **T** - Thoughts: Distract your mind with counting, planning, or a stimulating task.
- **S** - Sensations: Use intense physical sensations to interrupt the emotional experience.

DBT Skills for Life

"The journey of a thousand miles begins with one step."

- Lao Tzu

Maybe you're just starting your personal DBT journey, or maybe you've been using these skills for years. Wherever you are on your path, I want to let you know - this work is lifelong. The amazing part? You will always keep getting better at it.

When I was at my lowest point, struggling just to make it through each day, I never thought I'd be where I am now. DBT gave me so many tools to transform my life and my mindset. It has the power to bring you from actively planning your death to truly believing your life is worth living. It is a long road, but so worthwhile.

When I started DBT a few years ago, I had no idea how much it would transform my life. Just getting through each day used to feel impossible. Now, I can manage tough emotions without shutting down. It's been life-changing...and it keeps getting even better!

As I have told you before, 1 in 5 teens in the U.S. struggle with mental health issues. Maybe you also feel depressed or anxious from time to time. If yes, then you're not alone in feeling overwhelmed or like things will never get better. But I'm living proof that they can. With consistency and commitment to yourself, DBT can help you overcome any challenge and build the happy, fulfilled life you deserve.

These skills become second nature with practice. So, whenever you're struggling, have faith that you have the power within to lift yourself up and keep powering forward. Your best days are always still ahead, so don't give up on discovering them. You've got this - I believe in your ability to grow into the amazing person you're meant to be. Keep going!

DAILY DEEDS: FUN, FAST ACTIVITIES TO APPLY SKILLS IRL

Want to transform what you know into consistent growth? These quick, simple activities put the problems and solutions to the test. Give them a try – to meet your best self!

1. **Take the First Tiny Step:** Put the "big change" myth to rest. Commit to one small daily improvement, like drinking more water or stretching for 2 minutes. Watch how rapidly even baby steps add up over weeks without overwhelm. Share your mini win with friends to stay motivated!

2. **Plan Your Path:** Beat ambiguity with action! Craft a weekly schedule detailing when and how you'll focus, exercise, and socially recharge. Post it where you'll see it daily. Watch accountability help you stay on track even during busy times.

3. **Turn Triggers into Training:** Take notes on a favorite personal development podcast. Then set related triggers, like listening again in the car each week. Boost retention and see past lessons stay current longer term. Trigger to win!

4. **Remember to Remember:** Test your knowledge recall with weekly personal development trivia. Quiz your brain on interesting facts and keep retaking until you perfectly remember the answers to build mental muscle. Load the gains!

Progress, Not Perfection

Don't stress if you slip up sometimes. We're all works in progress. I still struggle, just less often. And just like leveling up in a video game, each success makes you stronger. You've got this!

Advice From Experience

"The price of anything is the amount of life you exchange for it."

- Henry David Thoreau

Consistency is key - don't quit practicing skills during tough times. They're meant for exactly when you're feeling overwhelmed. And remember, messy notebooks are better than no notebooks. Any effort puts you closer to your best self.

I'm proof that with DBT, you truly can overcome anything. My life today is way better than I ever dreamed it could be. Now it's your turn - trust the process, be patient with yourself, and keep powering through to your next level of greatness! Where will your DBT journey take you?

WANNA BE A SOCIAL BUTTERFLY? SCIENCE SAYS DBT CAN HELP!

Feeling awkward or anxious around others? You're not alone. But here's the cool thing: A study published by the National Institutes of Health (NIH), the top biomedical research agency in the world, found that teens who practiced DBT skills for just a few months showed significant improvements in their social interactions. They reported feeling more confident, assertive, and able to build stronger relationships. Pretty mind-blowing, right? So, what are you waiting for?

You've come so far in your DBT journey. While this chapter may be concluding, your journey of self-improvement is just beginning. Remember that cultivating your mental well-being is a lifelong process, and these skills will serve you well for years to come. Whenever challenges arise, you now have the powerful DBT toolbox to help you navigate intense emotions, build strong relationships, and regulate your reactions in healthy ways.

You now have the tools and knowledge to deal with whatever

life throws at you in terms of intense emotions. I'm so proud of all the progress you've made. Keep practicing, keep cultivating greater awareness of yourself and your skills, and continue surrounding yourself with support. You've got this - I can't wait to see how far your DBT journey will take you!

Key Takeaways

- Change offers opportunities for self-improvement.
- DBT provides strategies to guide your life positively.
- Consistent use of DBT skills helps build a confident, resilient future.
- Recognizing and celebrating small achievements boosts motivation and confidence.
- Simple acts like jotting down victories or treating yourself help maintain positive momentum.
- Mindfulness: Stay present and aware to develop your "wise mind."
- Interpersonal Effectiveness: Learn to assert your needs, set boundaries, and maintain healthy relationships.
- Distress Tolerance: Use coping mechanisms to handle tough emotions.
- Emotional Regulation: Take charge of your emotions using various techniques.
- Regularly practice DBT skills to make them second nature.
- Treat your DBT skills like tools to use consistently.
- Start with small changes and detailed plans.
- Use notes and reminders to apply skills in stressful moments.
- DBT is a lifelong journey with ongoing improvement.
- Consistent practice during tough times strengthens your ability to manage emotions and challenges.
- Don't stress over slip-ups; focus on continual progress.
- Consistency and patience are crucial for long-term growth.
- DBT has the power to transform lives if practiced diligently.

- Trust the process, be patient, and keep practicing to discover your best self.

CONCLUSION

WOW, IT'S HARD to believe we've reached the end of this DBT skills guidebook already. This book was meant to provide you with a comprehensive overview of the powerful coping strategies that make up DBT.

As I hope you've seen from the chapters, mindfulness, emotion regulation, interpersonal effectiveness, and distress tolerance are skills that can truly change lives when put into consistent practice. I'm so proud of each of you for taking this DBT journey with me and learning about new tools to help manage your stress, emotions, and relationships.

Let me quickly review some of the biggest lessons from each area we covered.

In mindfulness, we focus on living fully in the present moment through meditations, deep breathing exercises, and acting with awareness of our thoughts and surroundings. Emotion regulation taught the importance of understanding our feelings and having strategies like relaxation or opposite action to change their intensity if needed. Interpersonal effectiveness provided healthier communication tactics like DEAR MAN, GIVE, and validation to connect productively with others. For distress tolerance, we learned techniques like TIPP, self-soothing activities, and reality acceptance to withstand uncomfortable times rather than making them worse.

But here's the thing - this self-improvement journey doesn't end when you close this book. In fact, it's just beginning. DBT is a lifelong practice, not something you ever "complete." The more you keep using these skills, the more naturally they'll start to flow. And trust me, that's when the real magic happens.

I know, I know — the idea of consistently practicing new habits can feel daunting. Like, do I really have to keep meditating and journaling and all that stuff forever? The answer is a BIG yes. But hear me out. This isn't about piling on more work or meeting impossible standards. It's about investing in yourself, one small step at a time.

Think about it like leveling up in your favorite video game. The more you practice those combos and special moves, the stronger your character gets. Before you know it, you're taking down bosses that used to give you nightmares. Well, your brain is kinda like that video game character. The more you use these DBT skills, the more they'll become second nature. And that's when you'll really start to see the benefits in your everyday life.

So, let's talk about what those benefits look like. When you make DBT a regular part of your routine, you'll start to notice some incredible changes. For one, you'll feel more in control of your emotions. No more getting completely overwhelmed by stress or anxiety - you'll have a toolbox of strategies to lean on. Imagine how much easier school, social life, and relationships will be when you can stay cool, calm, and collected.

And speaking of relationships, your interpersonal effectiveness skills are going to skyrocket. You'll be able to stand up for yourself, set healthy boundaries, and communicate your needs clearly. Bye-bye, drama! Your friends and family are going to be amazed at how much you've grown.

But perhaps most importantly, regular DBT practice is going to boost your overall well-being and confidence. When you can manage your emotions, tolerate distress, and build meaningful connections, you start to feel like the best version of yourself. And that's where the real magic happens. You'll be able to pursue your passions, take healthy risks, and create the life you truly want. How awesome is that?

I truly believe that if we commit to practicing these new DBT superpowers regularly, they will serve us so well both now and in the future.

I wanted to share with you all an inspiring success story I heard about a teenager who used DBT. John was struggling a lot with anxiety, anger issues, and difficult family relationships. However, after a few months in a DBT skills group, he began noticing tremendous changes in himself. He said practicing daily mindfulness while walking to class made him feel calmer. John also learned to use distress tolerance coping strategies like squeezing an ice cube to help manage stress at home. Now, his mood is much more stable, and his relationships have improved, all because of the tools he gained from DBT. His story gives me hope and shows that with commitment, these strategies can truly work wonders.

John's story is just one example of the incredible impact DBT can have. But I have no doubt that if you keep practicing these skills, you'll experience your own version of that transformation. It might look different, but the result will be the same - a happier, healthier, more resilient you.

Well, friends, this concludes our journey through this DBT guide together. But remember - this is just the beginning for you! Your potential is limitless, and keeping these skills sharp through regular practice will supercharge your abilities to handle whatever life brings you with confidence and grace.

I challenge each of you to keep cultivating your emotional intelligence by finding small ways to incorporate DBT techniques into your daily routines. Write down what resonates most and hold yourself accountable for trying new things when big emotions come up.

You've all got this! I can't wait to see how bright your future becomes. Keep shining - you deserve every success coming your way.

Make a Difference with Your Review
Empowering Teens through DBT Skills

Now you have everything you need to achieve emotional well-being; it's time to pass on your newfound knowledge and show other readers where they can find the same help.

Simply by leaving your honest opinion of this DBT skills guidebook on Amazon, you'll show other teens where they can find the information they're looking for and pass on their passion for these coping strategies.

Thank you for your help. DBT skills are kept alive when we pass on our knowledge – and you're helping us to do just that.

Click here to leave your review on Amazon.

leave a review

ABOUT THE AUTHOR

EMMA DAVIS is a woman who wears many hats. She is a clinical social worker, a therapist, and a financial advisor, as well as the author of Effective Anger Management for Teens.

Her books are aimed at teenagers, covering a diverse range of topics, including life and coping skills, DBT techniques, finances, puberty, developing a growth mindset, and career planning. She focuses on the unique challenges faced by adolescents in their emotional and physiological development, empowering readers with a strong foundation for understanding.

Emma draws on experience and knowledge from all her roles, as well as her experience as a mother, to guide young people through the difficult stage of adolescence. She runs a therapy practice and financial education agency tailored to teenagers, and has worked with a diverse range of young people facing different practical and emotional challenges. She also runs several online courses on cultivating interpersonal skills, gratitude, happiness, and joy, as well as 10 residential care facilities for adults with disabilities and mental health challenges, which also informs her work.

Emma is married with 9 children between the ages of 3 and 22. She enjoys spending time with her family, practicing jiu jitsu, and developing her skills in photography.

Helping Teens With Finances, Anger Management, Mental Health, And Future Life Planning

From

EMMA DAVIS

Available on Amazon or wherever books are sold

To learn more about helping teens with finances, anger management, mental health, and future life planning at

www.emmadavisbooks.com

BIBLIOGRAPHY

10 ways to create family Harmony. (2019, February 14). Vivian Morgan, MS, LCPC.

A Therapist Explains Why We Shut Down When Flooded with Big Emotions. (n.d.).

Ackerman, C. E., MA. (2024, February 20). 21 Emotion Regulation Worksheets & Strategies. PositivePsychology.com.

Adams, C. B. L., MD. (2024, January 22). Not all social/emotional learning programs work well in school settings. Psychology Today.

Almonte, V. (2023, June 30). Celebrating your milestones: Unlocking the motivational power of progress - WindowStill. WindowStill.

Altrogge , S. (2024, April 10). 14 morning and evening routines that will set up each day for success. Zapier.com.

Asif, S., Mudassar, A., Shahzad, T. Z., Raouf, M., & Pervaiz, T. (2020). Frequency of depression, anxiety and stress among university students. Pakistan journal of medical sciences, 36(5), 971–976.

Bay Area Mental Health. (2022, December 10). 4 steps from DBT that can boost your self-esteem. BayAreaMentalHealth.

Beck, C. (2024, January 6). How to validate yourself when others dismiss your trauma. Supportive.

Carmichael, C., PhD, & Carmichael, C., PhD. (2024, February 21). How to Understand Your Emotions: 13 Steps (with Pictures). wikiHow.

Chapman, A. L. (2006). Dialectical behavior therapy: Current indications and unique elements. Psychiatry (Edgmont), 3(9), 62.

Children Exposed to Violence | Office of Justice Programs. (n.d.). Office of Justice Programs.

Chiu, A., Falk, A., & Walkup, J. T. (2016). Anxiety Disorders Among Children and Adolescents. Focus (American Psychiatric Publishing), 14(1), 26–33. https://doi.org/10.1176/appi.focus.20150029

Cisneros, V. (2023, November 21). Unlocking Resilience: The transformative power of dialectical behavior therapy for teens - outside the norm counseling. Outside the Norm Counseling.

Clinic, C. (2024, April 30). Yes, there is such a thing as stress sickness. Cleveland Clinic.

Coaching, H. (2024, February 17). The advantages of having a support system: creating your own support network. Medium.

Colomeischi, A. A., Duca, D. S., Bujor, L., Rusu, P. P., Grazzani, I., & Cavioni, V. (2022). Impact of a School Mental Health Program on Children's and Adolescents' Socio-Emotional Skills and Psychosocial Difficulties. Children (Basel, Switzerland), 9(11), 1661.

DALAL, A. (2023, December 1). Master The Art Of Communication: 10 Common Communication Fails To Avoid. Coggno.com.

Darnell, D., Flaster, A., Hendricks, K. E., Kerbrat, A. H., & Comtois, K. A. (2019). Adolescent clinical populations and associations between trauma and behavioral and emotional problems. Psychological Trauma, 11(3), 266–273.

Divyanka. (2023, October 6). Positive Lifestyle Guide: 17 Life-Changing Habits for Positive Living — Miss Tea Positive. Miss Tea Positive.

Greenwald, A. (2020, August 21). DBT Exercises and Self Help: How to use communication in everyday. Empower Your Mind Therapy.

Grouport (2022, November 23). A Beginner's Guide to Dialectical Behavior Therapy Skills. Grouporttherapy.com.

Healthie Inc. (2024, April 22). 9 benefits of goal setting & management. Healthie Inc.

Herzog, R. (2021, November 2). Improving the Moment: DBT Skills for Stress Management. Centerforcbt.org.

Hickson, J. (2023, October 2). How to Deal With Rejection: 10 Ways to Move On. Choosingtherapy.com.

Hippe, H. (2023, March 20). 8 Mindfulness practices to reduce stress. Nystrom & Associates.

Ho, L. (2023, February 3). How to celebrate small wins to achieve big goals. Lifehack.

Indeed (2023, May 13). How to write an action plan to help you achieve your goals. Uk.Indeed.com.

Jun, L. J. (2022, September 2). 3 Ways to turn knowledge into action - ILLUMINATION - medium. Medium.

Kliem, S., Kröger, C., & Kosfelder, J. (2010). Dialectical Behavior Therapy for Borderline Personality Disorder: A Meta-Analysis Using Mixed-Effects Modeling. Journal of Consulting and Clinical Psychology, 78(6), 936-51. https://doi.org/10.1037/a0021015

Koskie, B. (2023, October 31). Depression Facts and Statistics. Healthline.

Kripalani, K. (2022, May 6). 6 Steps to Finding light in Dark Times - Beauty everywhere. Beauty Everywhere.

Life Stance Health (2020, June 2). What is the PLEASE Skill and How Can It Help? Behavioralhealthflorida.com.

Lindner, J. (2023, December 20). Teen Stress Statistics: Market Report & Data. Gitnux.org.

Linehan, M. (2014). DBT? Skills training manual. Guilford Publications.

Lmft, D. K. (2019, April 21). Reducing Conflicts with the THINK Skill — Mindsoother Therapy Center. Mindsoother Therapy Center.

Lorandini, J. (2024, March 5). 4 Ways mindfulness in DBT therapy helps you regulate emotions. Suffolk DBT.

Lpc-S, A. D. (2024, April 8). Dialectical Behavioral Therapy for Teens – a complete guide. Clearfork Academy.

Lynsky, J. (2018, January 10). 5 Key Ways to be Intentional About your Goal Setting. Jeweltoned.com.

Masood, S., & Us Sahar, N. (2014). An exploratory research on the role of family in youth's drug addiction. Health psychology and behavioral medicine, 2(1), 820–832.

McGovern, C. (2021, July 1). Creating a healthy routine using DBT therapy guidelines. Empower Your Mind Therapy.

Moore, M. (2022, July 7). 4 DBT skills for everyday challenges. Psych Central.

Morgan, V. (2014, November 8). 10 Ways to Create Family Harmony.

Morgan, V. (2014, November 8). Counseling for Individuals, Couples, Families. Vivianmorgancounseling.com.

MSEd, K. C. (2023, December 31). 5 key emotional intelligence skills. Verywell Mind.

New Harbinger Publications. (2011, December 26). What mindfulness and acceptance can do for your Self-Esteem. HuffPost.

Pattemore, C. (2021, June 3). 10 Ways to build and preserve Better boundaries. Psych Central.

Perry, E. (2022, December 21). Get to know yourself through the act of self-reflection. Betterup.com.

Relevance Recovery. (2023, November 22). Dialectical behavior therapy and Aftercare.

Roemer, L. (2022, December 11). 4 Ways to Respond Effectively to Our Intense Emotions. Psychologytoday.com.

S. (2017, September 13). DBT Distress Tolerance Skills: Your 6-Skill Guide to Navigate Emotional Crises. Sunrisertc.com.

Schenck, L. (2012, May 29). 5 Essential conflict management skills. Mindfulness Muse.

Schwantes, M. (2018, June 9). 6 Smart Ways People With Emotional Intelligence Respond When Their Buttons Are Pushed. Inc.com.

Smith, J. (n.d.). 5 ways to manage student stress. Prospects.ac.uk.

Smith, M., MA. (2024, February 5). Improving Emotional Intelligence (EQ). HelpGuide.org.

Stanford Medicine Children's Health (n.d.). Understanding the Teen Brain. Stanfordchildrens.org.

Sunrisertc (2018, March 26). DEAR MAN DBT Skill: The Most Effective Way to Make a Request. Sunrisertc.com.

Surviving a Crisis: Dialectical Behavior Therapy (DBT) distress tolerance skills. (n.d.). MentalHelp.net.

Tedeschi, R. G. (2021, August 31). Growth after trauma. Harvard Business Review.

The 6 Stages of Behavior Change: A How-To Guide. (n.d.).

Walsh, K. (2022, November 22). 5 steps to turn your pain into purpose. DailyOM.com.

Weintraub, J., Cassell, D., & DePatie, T. P. (2021). Nudging flow through 'SMART' goal setting to decrease stress, increase engagement, and increase performance at work. Journal of Occupational and Organizational Psychology, 94(2), 230-258.

West, D. M. (2021, September 11). Is Dialectical Behaviour Therapy (D.B.T.) Effective for Teens? Mindease.io.

Zandi, H., Amirinejhad, A., Azizifar, A., Aibod, S., Veisani, Y., & Mohamadian, F. (2021). The effectiveness of mindfulness training on coping with stress, exam anxiety, and happiness to promote health. Journal of education and health promotion, 10(1), 177.

Zeman, E. (2019, August 11). Managing Fear — Mindsoother Therapy Center. Mindsoother Therapy Center.

Made in the USA
Coppell, TX
17 December 2024

42841004R00098